PUBLIC

SPEAKING

Overcome Public Speaking Fear and Manage
Business Presentations by Learning Storytelling
Techniques

(Influence Anyone With You Persuasion Skills
and Build Rapport)

Nick Noonan

Published by Rob Miles

© **Nick Noonan**

All Rights Reserved

Conversation: Overcome Public Speaking Fear and
Manage Business Presentations by Learning Storytelling
Techniques (Influence Anyone With You Persuasion Skills
and Build Rapport)

ISBN 978-1-989990-11-7

Legal & Disclaimer

The information contained in this book is not designed to replace or take the place of any form of medicine or professional medical advice. The information in this book has been provided for educational and entertainment purposes only.

The information contained in this book has been compiled from sources deemed reliable, and it is accurate to the best of the Author's knowledge; however, the Author cannot guarantee its accuracy and validity and cannot be held liable for any errors or omissions. Changes are periodically made to this book. You must consult your doctor or get professional medical advice before using any of the suggested remedies, techniques, or information in this book.

Upon using the information contained in this book, you agree to hold harmless the Author from and against any damages, costs, and expenses, including any legal fees potentially resulting from the application of any of the information provided by this guide. This disclaimer applies to any damages or injury caused by the use and application, whether directly or indirectly, of any advice or information presented, whether for breach of contract, tort, negligence, personal injury, criminal intent, or under any other cause of action.

You agree to accept all risks of using the information presented inside this book. You need to consult a professional medical practitioner in order to ensure you are both able and healthy enough to participate in this program.

Table of Contents

Introduction

No matter who you are, and whatever it is that you are doing in life, being able to communicate is definitely one of the things that you should learn. After all, you wouldn't be able to tell people what you want or what they need to know if you don't know how to speak up—even just a bit.

Communication is also important when it comes to working in companies, excelling in school, and when it comes to speaking—whether socially, or during meetings, or public speaking engagements, and the like. When you have enough confidence in yourself, it would be easier for you to relate to people from all walks of life.

With the help of this book, you would learn various communication techniques that can help you get through life better, be an effective communicator, and make sure that you won't have a hard time speaking up. Read this book now to find out how. Thanks again for downloading this book, I hope you enjoy it!

Chapter 1: The Fear Of Public Speaking

Pericles. Abraham Lincoln. Winston Churchill. Mohandas Ghandi. John F. Kennedy. Nelson Mandela. Martin Luther King, Jr. And, most recently, United States President Barack Obama.

What do these noted personalities have in common?

They are exceptional public speakers.

Watch them on the podium, or any place where they stand before the listening public and they are able to command attention and engage their listeners. Just seconds into their speeches and they have a captive audience. It is as if they have been born to do it; that they are completely unafraid about addressing large crowds.

But even the most seasoned motivational speakers in recent times will admit that they, too, had a fear of public speaking. Clearly, if these great orators and speakers do have a fear of public speaking, they were able to overcome it and even rise above it to become some of the best speakers of all time.

Giving Your Fear A Name

Fear of public speaking is often identified to come in various forms. Some people call it "stage fright", while others refer to it with the more technical term *"glossophobia"*.

Glossophobia, which is also known as speech anxiety, is derived from the Greek word *glossa* (tongue) and *phobos* (dread or fear). It is the severe fear of public speaking or of speaking in general, and it is actually one of the most common phobias in the world today, with 75% of the population suffering from it, albeit in varying degrees. In fact, it is experienced by more people than claustrophobia (fear of enclosed or tight spaces), agoraphobia (fear of heights), and arachnophobia (fear of spiders).

4

Some manifestations of glossophobia include the following:

•Freezing up in front of any audience, even just one or two people;

•Dry mouth;

•Numbing on the hands and lower extremities;

•Nausea and dizziness;

•Weak and shaky voice;

•Stuttering and stammering;

•Shortness of breath;

•Trembling or excessive shaking;

•Excessive sweating and flushing (extreme embarrassment);

•Accelerated heart rate; and

•Panic attacks.

Experts even claim that the dread felt by some students about being called by the teacher to stand in class to answer a question is an early manifestation of glossophobia. This case is so severe that even the thought of speaking in public is enough to cause one to feel extreme anxiety and distress.

Stage fright, on the other hand, can be considered a milder form, or even a symptom, of glossophobia. This form of performance anxiety covers any type of activity that entails having to perform in front of an audience, and is not limited to public speaking.

Causes of Fear of Public Speaking

There are a number of reasons that can be blamed as the cause of one's fear of speaking in public.

•Traumatic experiences. It is possible that the person had an actual past experience of speaking in public and ending up having an extremely embarrassing moment. Kids or teens that had this kind of experience tend to shy away from having to be exposed in such a situation where the same experience has a possibility of being repeated.

•One's upbringing or environment while growing up. People who grew up in an environment that does not help build up their courage and confidence to deal with crowds or even having conversations with many people tend to lack confidence and have low self-esteem. As a result, they, too, will shun the idea of having to speak in public.

•Lack of familiarity with the concept of public speaking. People are afraid of what they are not familiar with. Those who have not been exposed to public speaking, even from the point of view of being in an audience, will naturally feel nervous when the tables are turned and they are forced into the spotlight, so to speak.

•Speech problems. Those who grew up having speech problems such as stuttering will also tend to be wary of speaking in public.

Mostly, it is on a case-by-case basis. The reason for one person being terrified about standing up in front of a crowd may be different from another person.

Chapter 2: Be Physically Prepared

Something that many people fail to appreciate with regard to any mental or intellectual undertaking is the importance of being physically prepared. All too often people spend all of their time and energy preparing their heart and mind for an event, all the while ignoring their body and its needs. Unfortunately, this usually results in them having a harder time than they would have had, had they paid equal attention to physical preparation. It is important to understand that your body has a direct impact on your mental health and wellbeing. The stronger your body is, the sharper your mind will be. Therefore, it is critical that you spend as much time preparing yourself physically as you do mentally. This chapter will reveal four methods for ensuring that your body provides all the energy you need to give the best presentation possible.

Get Plenty of Sleep

Countless scientific and medical studies have shown just how important sleep is to a person's overall health and wellbeing. When you are sleep deprived, you will struggle with basic activities, both of a physical and mental nature. For example, your ability to do manual labor diminishes as your body isn't rested and recovered from previous exertions. Additionally, things such as memory, problem solving skills and the ability to focus on the task at hand begin to suffer when you don't get enough sleep. These symptoms can appear after only one night of restless sleep, or where you simply didn't sleep for long enough. Over time, these symptoms will increase in frequency and intensity, creating all sorts of problems in everything you do.

The trick, therefore, is to make sure that you get plenty of sleep leading up to the day of your event. Many people make the mistake of thinking the night before is all that counts, however, this isn't true. If you are somewhat sleep deprived going into the night before the event your body will only begin to recover with a decent night's sleep. It won't be at peak performance the next day, only somewhat better. Therefore, it is critical that you get enough sleep each and every day for a whole week before the event. Only then will your body and mind be rested and refreshed enough so as to 'fire on all cylinders.' Some people choose to take a power nap before a performance, giving them a boost of energy as well as a clear mind. A ten minute nap is all it takes, so if you have the time and a quiet place, you should grab forty winks to give yourself that extra edge.

Have Water Available

Another way in which your body can affect your performance is in its reaction to the stress and anxiety you feel. Different people have different physiological reactions to stress, however, there are some reactions that are common for most, if not all people. One such reaction is dry mouth. Whenever a person becomes anxious or excited, their mouth tends to dry up, causing them to have a harder time speaking as a result. Needless to say, this isn't something you want to deal with while speaking before a crowd. Therefore, always make sure that you have plenty of drinking water on hand to counter dry mouth, and thus prevent the effects it would have on your performance. This will also help to keep your mouth from drying out due to talking more than normal. Even if you aren't nervous, the fact is that your mouth will dry out the more you talk, making any speech harder as time progresses.

While dry mouth is a big enough problem on its own when giving a speech or presentation of any kind, the fact is that it can increase anxiety as well as causing discomfort. After all, when you become self-conscious of how dry your mouth is, and how that dryness is affecting your speech pattern, your stress levels will begin to rise exponentially. Therefore, in addition to keeping you from 'smacking your lips' due to having no saliva, a glass of water will help to keep your stress levels in check, which makes it an invaluable tool for successful public speaking.

Always Remember to Breathe

Stress and anxiety can change a person's physiology in many different ways. One way, in particular, is that they can make you breathe more rapidly than normal. Furthermore, each breath you take will be shallower than normal, meaning that you aren't getting the normal amount of oxygen from your breathing. At first, this might not seem like a real problem, especially since most crowds are too far away to notice your breathing rate. However, the way you breathe can have profound effects on both your body and mind, effects that can be a nuisance at best and absolutely disastrous at worst. Shallow breathing can starve your body and mind of the oxygen they need to function normally. When your body is oxygen deprived you will begin to feel tired, even dizzy after a while if your breathing remains shallow for too long. In extreme cases people have been known to pass out as a result of not getting enough oxygen to their brain.

Needless to say, you don't want this happening to you!

The trick, therefore, is to pay attention to your breathing at regular intervals. You don't want to pay attention to each and every breath you take, as that would make it impossible to focus on your presentation. However, simply taking a second or two in between thoughts or at other natural stopping points in your speech to assess your breathing will be enough to keep you in control. If you notice that you are breathing too quickly, or even worse, that you are holding your breath, take a couple of deep, relaxing breaths to restore your regular breathing rate. Not only will this provide oxygen to your body and mind it will also help to release nervous energy at the same time, making it a win/win!

Exercise

Public speaking can take a huge toll on a person's body, more so than most people expect. Part of this is due to the fact that you will be standing for a long period of time, probably longer than you are used to standing in regular day-to-day life. While standing may not seem like a physically challenging activity, it can, in fact, drain your energy far more than you realize. Additionally, you may walk around more than normal, and you will probably speak in a louder voice than you usually use while speaking under normal circumstances. All of these things require far more energy than you might think, meaning that your body needs to be in good shape in order to handle the extra demands of public speaking.

In addition to plenty of sleep, it is essential that you get a decent amount of exercise leading up to your presentation. This doesn't mean that you have to run ten miles a day or go to the gym to lift weights, rather some brisk walking on a daily basis will be enough to increase your physical stamina significantly. As mentioned previously, breathing is a critical element when it comes to public speaking. Thus, any exercise that improves respiratory function will help to improve your body's ability to handle the task at hand. Rapid walking, taking the stairs instead of the elevator, or any other light exercise that increases air and blood flow will help to improve physical and mental performance, thus giving you a significant edge. For best results try to exercise thirty minutes each day for at least a week before your event, the same time frame as that of your improved sleep regimen.

Chapter 3: Characteristics Of A Strong Public Speaker

Strong public speakers work to develop characteristics that will enhance their ability to engage audiences in ways that are productive to all parties concerned.

Here is a list of characteristics that those who aspire to be excellent public speakers practice regularly:

A Strong Public Speaker is Organized – Talented public speakers understand the need for organization from preparation through presentation. Persuasive speeches need to be organized so that the theme of the argument is stated near the beginning of the speech and supported with reasoning that is easy to understand and to follow throughout the presentation. Informational speeches need to be organized in a way that the information is laid out logically and in an order that is comprehensible to the audience.

Not only do strong public speakers organize their speeches or presentations so that their audiences find them compelling – they also organize all their materials, including visual aids and equipment, their biography, and their handouts, so that they are readily available and ready to go to work for them when they need them.

A Strong Public Speaker is Prepared – Quality public speakers would never think of entering a situation that calls upon them to make a presentation without effectively preparing and practicing unless it was a last-minute situation. Those who value preparation take great care conducting necessary research for their speeches, making sure their data is organized in a logical and understandable format, and then practicing their speeches so that they know their presentations are as best as they can be.

Prepared public speakers have taken the time to learn as much as they can about their audiences so that they can tailor their speeches accordingly. In addition, they have taken the time to learn about the venues in which they will speak, as well as developed appropriate supplemental materials such as visual presentations, handouts and business cards so they enhance their presentations for audience members. Prepared presenters also make sure that their written material contain no spelling, grammar, or typographical errors in order to maximize the professionalism of their presentations. Speakers who are using technical equipment such as projectors or computers make sure that their equipment is in proper working order and that they have access to backups of parts that may fail during their presentations, such as projector bulbs.

A Strong Public Speaker Speaks with No Filler Words or Phrases – Filler words and phrases such as "um," "ah," "like," and "you know" are destructive because they distract your audience member's attention from your message. I recently attended a conference where a young lady spoke on a topic that held much interest for me, but I found myself counting how many times she said "um" and "like" instead of listening to the content of her speech! One of your main goals as a speaker is to rid your speech of filler words. Often, speakers have no idea that they are using filler words in their conversations, which is why you should have others critique your speech or record yourself on video or audio so that you can see where your weaknesses are in this area. Speakers tend to use more filler words when they are nervous, unprepared, or both. The better you know your material, the less likely that filler words will make their way into your presentation. People also use filler words in order to avoid silent pauses in their speech. Don't be afraid of silence. Listeners will rather have silence than listen to filler words.

A Strong Public Speaker Uses Clear and Precise Speech - Strong public speakers understand the importance of using clarity and precision as they present orally to their audiences. Vague words and phrases have no business in public speeches because they leave questions in the minds of the audience. Similarly, ambiguous speech, in which words and phrases may be interpreted more than one way, should also be avoided in public speech because they are unclear and thus may serve to confuse the listener. A strong public speaker uses language that is appropriate for his audience. If a speaker uses jargon, acronyms, or other unfamiliar terms in the speech, he takes the time to define those terms so that all audience members understand them.

A Strong Public Speaker is Well-Groomed - Public speakers who take their role seriously will make sure they dress appropriately the day they give their presentation. One's appearance speaks volumes, and if a presenter's clothes are inappropriate or if he or she has not taken the time to groom appropriately, the speaker's negative nonverbal message may speak louder and more memorably than the speech. This is one of the major reasons speakers need to learn as much as they can about the culture of the people to whom they will be speaking. Not every speaking situation calls for presenters to wear professional attire; however, speakers should always appear neat and clean and they should wear clothing that is appropriate for the occasion.

A Strong Public Speaker Engages the Audience - One of the most important skills public speakers should master is learning how to "connect" with the audience. Effective public speakers are aware of how their use of body language, including eye contact, can work to grab the attention of their audiences. Using appropriate hand gestures and body movement can accentuate main points made in a presentation. Most people enjoy making eye contact with others, and no one likes to listen to a speech when the speaker reads from papers or notes and never looks up. Strong public speakers engage their audience members by looking at them as they speak. Obviously, speakers probably will not have the opportunity to latch eyes with each audience member if they are speaking to one hundred people, but

23

everyone in the audience will appreciate it if they see the speaker making the effort to make eye contact when they can do so.

Another method strong public speakers can use to build rapport between themselves and their audience members is to use a question-and-answer format for a part of the presentation. Often, audience members will enjoy the opportunity to ask a question or make a comment regarding the presentation; this offers an opportunity for meaningful dialogue between the presenter and the audience. Strong public speakers realize, though, that if they are going to take questions from the audience, they should prepare for this by anticipating possible questions and then designing appropriate responses.

A Strong Public Speaker is Aware of the Power of the Voice – As trained oral communicators, strong public speakers understand that the voice is a very important instrument of delivery. To get the most out of the use of that instrument, speakers must practice using it just like they would practice using any other instrument. Speakers who speak clearly and who are able to vary the pitch and the volume of their voices can use it to emphasize salient points of their presentations and to hold audience attention.

A Strong Public Speaker Understands the Power of Humor - There are probably a handful of situations when it would be totally inappropriate to use humor in a speech (George W. Bush's speech to the American citizenry following the events of September 11th, 2001 comes to mind), but they are few and far between. Humor breaks up the tedium of a speech and may serve to strengthen that connection between presenter and audience members discussed previously. When speakers consider using humor, though, they should make sure that it is appropriate to the audience to which they are presenting.

A Strong Public Speaker Researches the Venue – It may not always be possible for speakers to visit the location where they are scheduled to speak ahead of time, but they should find out as much as they can about the size and the layout of the room and available equipment well before the day of their scheduled presentation. In addition, they should know exactly how they are going to get there the day of the presentation. It's never, ever a good idea to show up late to a speaking engagement. In fact, it's a great idea to plan on arriving to speaking venues at least an hour early so that speakers can check out the layout, make sure the technical equipment is in good working order, and breathe a bit before show time.

A Strong Public Speaker Researches His Audience - No matter how speakers end up being charged with presenting speeches in front of others, it is going to be very important for speakers to learn as much as they can about the people who will be in attendance as they present. The more speakers know about their audiences, the better they will be able to tailor their presentations so that their audiences can derive maximum benefit from the information the speakers will provide them. If at all possible, speakers should know some basic demographic information regarding audience members including age range and gender, as well as reasons they are gathering.

Questions to Ponder:

1. What are your strengths as a public speaker?
2. What characteristics of a strong public speaker do you need to practice and

develop to strengthen your skills as an oral communicator?

Chapter 4: The Monomyth Explained: A Storytelling Template That Has Survived The Test Of Time

In the previous chapter, we briefly touched on the idea of "crescendos" in your speech. The idea that your delivery should never be stagnant, but vary as your performance unfolds. The idea that your speech should have a certain *rhythm.*

This concept also makes up the backbone of story-telling in general. If you embed the correct "emotional candor" into the content of your speech itself, an engaging delivery will naturally follow suit.

It just so happens, there's a hundred-thousand-year-old "template" for doing just that. It is a template for telling stories that speak to the essence of humanity.

Homer used it. Tolkien used it. George Lucas used it. Countless public speakers, politicians, and stand-up comedians the world over use it every day, and you can use it too.

I am speaking of what Joseph Campbell calls "The Monomyth." The monomyth describes a way to structure the plot of a story so that it engages and inspires an audience to great effect. Let's break it down.

How an Epic and Inspiring Hero's Journey Unfolds in Three Easy Acts

(Note: This is a highly condensed and streamlined version of the classical hero's journey outlined by the monomyth. For a full in-depth analysis, check out Joseph's Campbell's bestselling book *The Hero with a Thousand Faces.*)

ACT ONE: Our "Hero's tale" almost always begins with the protagonist in a slump. They're either bored to death with their hum-drum life or outright suffering in squalor.

Maybe they're not a very nice person, or maybe they are but they can't catch a break. Either way the gist of this segment is that something isn't right. The hero isn't living the life he wants to live, even if he can't quite put his finger on why.

Then, something happens to shake the hero out of their stupor: an unexpected event that pushes them out of their comfort zone and kicks off a metamorphosis. They may be resistant to the changes in their life at first, and they may or may not come upon a mentor-like figure who will guide them through their transformation.

Now the stage is set, the ball sent rolling, and the journey begun.

Soon, the hero eases into their new circumstances and starts to make some small gains on their position in the world.

But almost equally as soon come's an event Campbell calls "crossing the threshold." Here the hero's commitment to the long journey before them is put to the test. Here they must conquer some "unknown" challenge that arises.

The successful "crossing of the threshold" concludes Act One. Now, the training wheels have been removed and there's no going back for our hero.

ACT TWO: In the next leg of the journey, our hero begins to see some real progress towards their goal. Now they start to become real "players" in the game of their endeavor, so to speak. New allies are met, and new challenges arise which the hero overcomes.

But just when things are starting to look like gravy, "the ordeal" rears its ugly head. The ordeal is an elephant-sized problem that makes Act One's threshold look like small potatoes. It shatters the hero and appears to undo everything they've gained so far.

Now, the audience spends some significant time with the hero at his or her worst. They feel the hero's pain.

Act Two concludes with the hero at his lowest point yet, questioning whether they would have been better off if they never embarked on the journey to begin with. If the hero had a mentor figure in the story, they've most likely lost access to his or her valuable guidance by this point.

ACT THREE: The final act revives the plot with a spark of inspiration that carries the hero out of their despair. Here something almost magical occurs that prompts our protagonist to resume their noble cause.

Back on the journey's path, the hero—having suffered great injury from Act Two's ordeal—finds progress more difficult than ever. Every inch forward is a battle, but their strength of spirit has returned, and the audience is rooting for them every step of the way.

At this point, the hero might need to attain some form of hidden knowledge or power that will allow them to triumph over the ordeal. Here, a second transformation occurs: a re-forging and redoubling of the first great change that set them on their path to begin with.

This prepares the hero for their final confrontation with the ordeal.

But what sort of dramatic confrontation would it be if the hero's victory was assured? As the final conflict begins, the audience is made to realize that the ordeal, too, has grown even more problematic since the hero's initial defeat, downfall, and hard-earned rebirth.

The hero now squares off against the "supreme ordeal" here at the ultimate climax of the story, and the stakes have never been higher.

The hero, of course, comes out of the finale triumphant. But their triumph is probably bitter-sweet, as they've most likely lost something very dear to them in the process of overcoming their ordeal. Overall, however, their end goal has been achieved, and their long and difficult transformation a success.

Finally, the hero returns to their place of origin—a changed and better person—and share the spoils of their victory with the less fortunate. And so, the hero's journey ends—in a sense—exactly where it began, and the cycle is complete.

A Very Simple Example of the Monomyth in Action

See now, how the monomyth can be harnessed to deliver a seemingly mundane happening as though it were a life-changing sequence of events—all leading up to a profound and memorable conclusion...

ACT ONE: I'd been working 50 hour weeks at the office for five years straight. My eyes felt like they were about to fall out of their sockets for lack of natural sunlight.

Driving home one day, those tired eyes of mine saw the cutest baby squirrel on the side of the road...flattened like a pancake. I saw that, and that's when it hit me. Our time on this earth is just too short. I decided that I needed to get out of the office and clear my head. Center myself. Figure out what I'm doing with my life.

I booked a spot on a nearby campground for the weekend. Just me and the great outdoors for 48 hours straight.

But naturally, my boss paid a visit to my cubicle on the Friday before my trip.

"We need you here for the Peterman account this weekend," he said. "I hate to ask again, but I know we can always count on you for— "

"—NO." I cut him off, eyes bulging. Beneath my desk, I could feel my hands balling up into fists.

My boss looked absolutely thunderstruck.

"NO." I told him again. He looked at me. I looked at him. I must have looked like a crazy person, because he didn't say another word. He just backed on out of the cubicle and went his way.

ACT TWO: The first couple hours of roughing it were great. I hit the trails right away—went for a nice, long walk. I breathed in clean, fresh air; stretched out all my aching muscles. Already, I was starting to feel like a whole new person.

But then night fell, and disaster struck.

Turns out I'd locked my keys in the car. Not just my keys, mind you, everything. My cell phone. My tent. All my food and other essentials. Just a

Just then, I heard a *crack* in the distance. Thunder. Clouds had rolled in out of nowhere. In the next second, it was pouring down rain.

And what do you know what else? It just so happened this one of the last weekends that the campground was open for the season, and the whole place was practically abandoned.

I hiked a good two miles from where I was parked to the front help station, only to find that this post was just as empty as everywhere else. Great customer service, right?

All I could think to do was take shelter in the woods, and even that hardly helped, it was raining so hard. Freezing, soaked, huddled up in a ball against a big rotting stump, all I could think about was what a dummy I had been.

Right now, I could have been heading home from the office for an evening of nice, dry, temperature-controlled modern shelter.

Instead I was crouched here like an animal at the world's worst campground. I thought, *how did I get this stupid camping idea into my head?*

ACT THREE: At some point I must have fallen asleep there in the woods. When I woke up, it was still dark, but at least the rain had stopped. The moon must have been about full that night because I could still make out the trail just fine.

I knew I needed to get moving or I'd probably catch pneumonia from sitting their soaked clothing. Should I go back to my car and try to bust the window open? I decided that I would go further along the trail, keeping an eye out for a suitable rock to do the job.

I kept up along the trial for some time, toes growing numb in my shoes, until I came unto to a big muddy pond. It was the campground's fishing hole I guess. I plopped down on a log to rest for a while before I headed back. And just when I did, that's when it happened. A moment in time that would change my life forever.

The sun rose.

All at once those golden, pink and orange hues started dancing on the dirty, mucky pond. Lit it up like a canvas of neon. And while this pond is transforming into something wonderful—while I'm sitting here on a log, haven't eaten in a day, covered in mud, eyes dried up like some raisins because I slept in my contacts...allI'm thinking is: this is so...beautiful.

And then I realize, I've never done this. I've never watched a sunrise. Not once. Not even when I was kid. My dad wasn't the type to take us on early morning fishing trips, he was too busy...working...

...but hell, who am I to hold that against him? When he was my age he already had a wife and kids. Me? I've been too busy working to even get that much out of life...

So there I am, looking out at the most beautiful sunset I've ever seen (the only one I've seen, to be fair), filthy and tired here at the world's worst campground, thinking all these things...and I start to tear up. But you know what? They're tears of joy.

Because now I feel like some curse has been lifted. Now I feel awake. And as I head back to my campground, I'm not worried about my situation with my car, because all I can think is "What else have I missed?

What other beautiful things have been under my nose this whole time, things that I've been too busy working to appreciate?"

So I get back to my car and you know what's the first thing I see? Something shiny embedded in the dirt by my tire. I didn't lock my keys in my car, I missed dropping them in my pocket.

Why had I not noticed? Because I was too busy with the task of *unbusying* myself when I got out of the car for the weekend.

I called in sick that Monday. Took the next Friday off, then following week entirely. I read some books I had been meaning to read for years. I went out. Made new friends.

Then I came back to work more refreshed than any weekend in the woods by itself could have done for me.

And the first thing I told my boss when I got back? I told him how we ought to have a company camping trip.

Making the Monomyth Work for You

You've just read but one, very quick, very loose example of the monomyth in action.

I'm sure you noticed that the story hardly followed the monomyth to a T. There was no mentor involved, nor did the plot's ordeal up the ante toward the end of our hero's journey.

Still, the broad brush strokes of the journey were there, and the made what could have been an entirely uninteresting story into something impactful.

Once you've memorized the beats of the monomythic hero's journey, you start to see it everywhere. In modern fiction. In TV and movies. Even on a micro scale in commercials, print ads, and product branding.

Once you've absorbed the monomyth completely, you'll start to wonder how it's possible to tell a good story *without it*. It works so well, perhaps, because it's the most obvious way of structuring a meaningful plot.

As I said before, there are no rules when it comes to speech writing, only guidelines. So, too, is the structure of the monomyth nothing more than an effective set of guidelines for telling stories to your audience. Feel free to add your own flair to the formula, but there's also no need to reinvent the wheel.

Chapter 5: How To Study The Bible

Reading to Understand the Bible (Is a journey)

Reading to understand the Bible and studying the Bible are similar concepts. Understanding a Bible verse us understanding the context. This involves reading around the verse and understanding the bigger picture. Studying the verse involves taking the context and researching it. These two concepts take time and involve patience. It is always good to journal the process of understanding the context of a Verse. At the same time, it is good to keep track of researching the context.

You shouldn't cut verses in half and just use what sounds good when you are sharing what you found in the Bible. This goes for everything we use as a reference. If you walk into a room and overhear two friends talking about something, things can easily be misunderstood you hear half of the conversation and don't understand the context. This is where gossip is started. He said this or she said this. The same way is for quoting things from the Bible. Make sure that you know what the Bible is talking about, and what the author means in the context. Reading around the verse can be quite a journey of discovery. We can share the journey of finding verse when we get up to talk.

Questions you are going to want to understand are:

Who wrote the passage and what was their life like?

Who was the passage written to and what were the circumstances?

Was it written before Jesus came or after his resurrection?

The Bible is a story about Jesus. The Old Testament was pointing to the need of Jesus and the New Testament points to newness of life that following Jesus offers. Understanding this can help in the process of understanding the Bible and Scripture that is used to talk about.

I cannot stress enough that you shouldn't use a phrase or half of a Bible verse. Don't mold a verse to say what you want it to. Make sure that you explain the Bible as it is written and not as you think it should be written. There are many warnings in the Bible of people who misrepresent what the Bible says.

What is a cross-reference and how to use it in your Sermon?

A cross-reference is a term used when a bible verse or passage says the same thing somewhere else in the bible. Cross-references are used to help explain a concept in the bible and bring clarity to what the Bible means on a topic. When the books of the Bible were put together to form the Bible one of the requirements was a number of cross-references with other books. Most bibles will provide footnotes to help the reader find footnotes related to different chapters. Keep in mind that even when you are using a suggested cross-reference that you should still 'read to understand' every reference you plan to use in your Sermon.

How to Study Scripture
2 Timothy 3:16-17 (New International Version)
"All Scripture is God-breathed and is used for teaching, rebuking, correcting and training in righteousness, so that the servant of God may be thoroughly equipped for every good work."

I remember a high school teacher telling the class a quote on my first day of Grade 12. She said; "You have time for the things you make time for" – Unknown Author. This is something that has stuck with me through the years. When we study anything, we have time for what we make time for. How to study the Bible is choosing to make time.

There are many ways to study the Bible. The first thing I like to do is get a bible and notepad. Sometimes people like getting a thesaurus or dictionary for words that are not understood. The second thing I do, read the chapter and write out the verse or passage that I want to use. As you read the chapter, keep track of verses that stand out to you; before and after the passage that you want to use. I also like to keep track of cross-references that might be suggested in the chapter. I like to write out a summery of the entire chapter, and then write out a summery of the specific verse or passage I want to use for my sermon. I like writing out ways that I can apply the scripture to my life. Lastly I like to pray about the Verse asking God to help me understand and apply the Verse.

It is important to not take the scripture out of context. As you study the Bible, you will learn to take your time and not rush through Bible Verses. Cross-referencing is very helpful to understand a concept. Memorizing scripture can also help you know a Verse and keep it on your mind. Sometimes when we memorize things, it helps us live them out. The Bible is meant to be a meditation tool to teach, rebuke, correct, and for training in righteousness as it talks about in 2 Timothy 3:16-17. Every time we read or share the Bible has that effect on its audience; to teach, rebuke, correct, and train in righteousness. However you might mean to preach, it will be received in one of those four ways. Everyone is different and everyone will receive scripture in different ways.

Memorizing Scripture – Explained with Sample Memorization Tools Attached

I'd like to explain some simple ways to easily memorize. Memorizing something really is a self-taught class. We use our memory everyday. Find some space to yourself and grab a notepad. Try to set yourself up not to be distracted by the busyness of life. Remember, if you were in a class at school you would have very little distractions. Try to create the same environment when you are trying to learn these new tips and tricks for memorizing. The examples that I am providing are just a few that are easily explained in my book; "How to Memorize Scripture".

a)   Example 1: How to Memorize Scripture

The easiest way and most redundant way to memorize something is to read the verse. Read it again. Read it again. Read it again. Read it again. Read it again. Read it again. Read it again. Read it again. Read it again. Read it again. Read it again. Read it again. Read it again. Is it memorized yet? Repetition is annoying, but it is easy, and it does work.

b)   Example 2: How to Memorize Scripture

Another way to memorize Scripture is turning it into a song. This requires a little more work then just reading the verse over and over again. If you are musically inclined it will be easy for you to turn the Scripture Verse into a song you can easily memories to a tune.

c)   Example 3: How to Memorize Scripture

One way you can memorize Scripture is by cutting out each line like a puzzle. I would suggest that you don't do this with the pages of your Bible. It works much easier with some paper from a notepad. Write out the Bible Verse and then cut out each line of the Scripture Passage. Then take out a line and try again. Repeat this exercise until you can say the entire Verse without seeing it.

d)   Example 4: How to Memorize Scripture

Find a friend and play charades. Go through the Verse and try to get the other person to guess each word as you act it out. This is a great activity and will help you memorize the verse in no time.

Chapter 6: Overcome Your Fears

"The problem with speeches isn' t so much not knowing when to stop, as knowing when not to begin."

When it comes to speaking in public, it has been said that the reason why more people don't do it is because it's actually one of the top fears in the world, next to death.

Let's think this through. Take a look at today's wealthiest people. In most cases, to obtain wealth they've had to have great communication skills. It doesn't matter if you are speaking to a set of executives or to thousands, if you can't be effective with your communication, it will absolutely affect your bottom line.

I know some of you will say, "well I can actually hire someone to speak for me, right?" Yes, this is true. However, that person has to be effective. Typically, it's that person who will become the face of the company. It's that person people will remember. That is the person who truly makes the impact in the world.

Look at Steve Jobs and his story. He wasn't the programmer, he was the visionary communicator for the company. It is Steve Jobs that most people think of when they think of Apple. Although he wasn't the one actually designing the devices, he was the one who delivered them to the world.

I meet so many entrepreneurs who want to have that type of impact. Maybe not necessarily impacting the millions like Steve Jobs did, but impacting them on some level. To do that, you will have to get over the fear of speaking in public. While I won't be able to go into everything in regards to getting rid of your fears, I believe this chapter will get you started.

If you want a more in-depth book on eliminating your fears, I recommend you get my book *Fear – 10 Steps to Letting Go of Your Fears,* which is located on my website www.ShowYourSuccess.com under STORE. Trust me, it will be a great companion with this book if you have any fears.

Write down how this fear is affecting your business

Now the first thing you have to do is be willing to address the fears that are affecting your business. Write them down on paper. For example, is it the fear of ridicule? The fear of rejection? What specifically is the fear that is affecting you?

The next thing you need to do is write down what will or will not happen as a result of having this fear. If you allow this fear to affect your actions, what will it keep you from? Is this fear costing your business money?

The truth is, you don't have fears about actions... you have fears about results. It's not that you are afraid of speaking in public, you are afraid of what will happen to you if you take that action. You must figure this out, because if you never identify what this fear is, then it will be extremely difficult to push through it.

Personally, I had a fear of rejection and also I guess a fear of neglect. As a child, I just remember many times when I would speak, and no one would listen. I remember the frustration that I used to have from that. This caused me to seriously go silent and become shy. Well, I no longer have that challenge. Do I still think about it every now and then? Yes, of course. However, I do not allow that fear, or even the thought of it, to keep me from taking the action of speaking. Being shy was just keeping me broke.

Join a speaking group

I have to be honest, I didn't really join a speaking group myself. Instead, I enrolled in three different speaking courses where I hired a coach to work with me. I preferred the one-on-one effect. Keep in mind, one-on-one coaching may cost you more money. A great way to determine if you want to go to that level is to join a group.

One of my courses did, however, register me to join a community of speakers, where we could present our talks and even get some advice. For me, this is always great because you can get feedback from other action takers. I'm just a big believer that you must spend your time in environments that inspire you.

In many of these groups you will get a chance to learn so many technical things as well, which will help you as a speaker. For example, things like how to position your hands. Some people don't realize that their movements on a stage can affect their talk. There are just so many things that we could discuss, but some of the best ways to learn your information and practice is within a group of other speakers. I do also have a chapter on some of these ideas to help you along the way.

In regards to your fears, joining speaking groups will help you tremendously. I always feel more brave when I'm around other people who are pushing through the same fears that I have.

I remember many times when I was dealing with my fear of meeting new people, I would always ask for others to come with me. These were people who were business minded. These were people who learned themselves how to meet people one on one and build relationships. When I spent time with these kinds of people, I would always feel more confident.

Joining a speaking group will also help you to get more comfortable. It will allow you to practice, and I promise you this, the more you do your talk, introduction, speech, etc., the more you will build your confidence.

Acknowledge those fears

Now that you have written down your fears, you must be willing to acknowledge them. As I mentioned before, write them down and then identify what they are costing you. You may even need to dig a bit further and figure out when these fears started. In most cases, it started when you were a child. There was something that happened to you that caused you to develop these feelings and insecurities. The key to overcoming anything is being willing to acknowledge it and then take the proper actions steps to move on.

I'm a big believer that we choose to be who we are. We choose to accept the fact that we are shy. We choose to accept the fact that we don't like talking in front of people. I know some people may say… "Taurea, you are wrong! I did not choose to be shy."

I don't mean to offend anyone, but think about that statement. I'm serious about this. If you didn't choose to be shy, then don't. We have free will.

We are able to choose to be whoever we want. With repetition, you are able to change those habits. Being shy is nothing but a learned behavior, and the actions you take to reaffirm that behavior come through your habits. If you want change, you must change.

Talk about what you know

A top reason that most people are afraid to speak in public is because they don't want to look silly. Well, the best way to not look silly is to make sure you are talking about something you know about.

I remember when I first started speaking in front of groups like it was yesterday. I had no clue what I was talking about. I had just joined this company and we were supposed to share a testimonial. I had no idea what I was doing. I was so scared that you could see my clothes moving because of my trembling.

I was horrified, but at the same time, I was so excited about what I was about to do, so I decided to take a chance and see what would happen.

I wasn't as successful as I might have liked right away, but eventually I began to really get good. I started investing in public speaking courses and growing my strength in communication even more. The best purchases I've ever made were investing in public speaking courses and book-writing courses. In fact, they were so good that now I actually teach those very topics!

I've seen how being a great communicator and how having great tools can truly elevate your business to another level. The key is to know what you're talking about. So if you're starting off and maybe you don't know as much as you'd like, just start and continue to educate yourself. You will get better and better.

Now I want to answer this question, because I know you are thinking it: "Should I wait to start until I learn more about my topic?" I will say no. The reason is that things, concepts, and ideas are always changing. It will never be a perfect time to get started. Because this is true, there is no reason not to get started now. Trust me, all you can do is get better and better.

Chapter 7: How To Banish Fears Of Public Speaking

We talked about stage fright and nerves in the last module and as this is an important part of public speaking, it's important to understand where nerves come from and how they will affect you. Nerves of course stem from fear. It is the fear of not knowing what the outcome will be but also includes the following:

Fear   of   being   judged
•   Fear   of   being   ridiculed

- Fear of making a mistake
- Fear of being criticized
- Fear of not being a success

Fear can be debilitating if you let it. The ridiculous thing about fear is that it causes nervousness about an event that has yet to happen and so, we must rationalize our fears and to consider what we are really frightened about.

Once you realize that your source of fear is the inability to see ahead to an outcome, it does empower you. The fears are not real and so, there is no point worrying about them. Fear can work for you instead of against you however. It can give you an adrenalin rush and help you to become more dynamic in your approach. Nerves are not a sign of lack of confidence. Visualize yourself in complete control when you step out on that stage and think of them as YOUR audience.

Tip
Remember that most people in the audience want you to succeed and are there to learn something or be entertained. They are for the most part on your side already.

The key to banishing your fears is to be authentic. By being yourself, you attract the right people to you and people see the real you. It is also much easier to just be yourself, anything else is acting and that requires a skill. At all times, relax and be yourself. Nerves may plague you initially but, know this, once you start talking, you will overcome them quickly and, you will enjoy your time in the spotlight.

Fear stands for "False evidence appearing real"

Being Prepared

When you are fully prepared it takes away some fears quite naturally. You may still feel butterflies in the stomach but, that's okay. We talked previously as to how celebrities may feel prior to an event and how, they have to learn to deal with their nerves too. It can help to motivate or to psych you up and, will provide you with an adrenalin rush. It is only when fears become irrational that it leads to a problem. Your hands may shake, your knees feel a little wobbly and your lips may feel dry, but this is all very natural. You must face your fears and walk out on that stage and give the best performance you can.

Rehearsing everything over and over really will help you to feel less nervous as you know you can rely on yourself to deliver a speech that has been well-rehearsed. Providing you know that fear is only in your thoughts and that it does not dictate the outcome, you can let it go. If you are visualizing and creating positive thoughts, then, the outcome will almost certainly be the same. Practice breathing techniques to help calm your mind if your nerves start to jangle. By doing so, you slow down your heart rate, and still the mind.

Once you know the material you are going to cover is imprinted on your mind, then, it's time to take it a stage further and to make a detailed plan. Write down headers that prompt you. Associate passages of your speech with those headers. These will form a back-up prompt should you forget your place.

Tip
Never be frightened to add something in as you speak live. Sometimes these spontaneous moments can be the highlight of the speech.

Breathing Techniques

Before you walk out and start to deliver your speech, utilize some very simple breathing techniques that will help slow your heartrate down and generally instill some calm into your persona. By breathing very deeply and slowly, you will quite naturally slow your thoughts which may be whizzing around your head at a hundred miles an hour at this point. This method really works in slowing everything down and creating a calmer and more relaxed you. Remember that everyone feels nerves and that is nothing to fear. Countless thousands of people have felt the same fears as you and this includes top politicians and other well-known public speakers.

Relaxation techniques are often the key to releasing built-up tension. You will see so many people using different methods to accomplish this. Some will listen to music, others will practice yoga or, tell jokes. Some people use affirmations to build up their confidence levels and to calm them. It really is a case of finding out what suits you the best.

People Can't See Your Fear

If you think that people can tune into your own nervous feelings, you are wrong. As you walk out with your stomach all knotted, they have no idea how you feel inside. If you think people are in tune with how you feel this will make you more nervous. If you stand tall with your shoulders back, chest out and your posture good, then, people will assume you are confident and in control. This has a duel effect as you will feel more confident too when you improve your posture and stride out onto the stage.

Audience Reaction

It is true that a polished speaker will be able to read his audience and be able to change the flow when needed by perhaps injecting a little humor or bringing in some interesting facts. However, this is something that occurs over time. You can't possibly please everyone all the time and nor should you worry about that. It does depend on the setting and the type of speech but there will always be the odd person in the audience who is distracted. There could be many reasons for this i.e. personal problem, an aching back, or, perhaps they did not want to attend. This has no reflection on your presentation. Some people in an audience will look a little bored or distracted irrespective of the topic or the delivery so do not overthink this. If you allow this to play on your mind, it will eat into your confidence, which in turn will create more nerves the next time you are asked to do a public speech.

Work hard to engage your audience and try to make sure your presentation is interesting – whether using PowerPoint or, standing at a podium free-talking. Built a connection, make eye contact with some people, smile, do not rush your words, add emphasis to them. You might even be able to fit in a slot where people can ask questions, and this is always a good way to build a link to your listeners.

Wrong Words, Right Words.

Your ability to get your message across to a crowd of people can often balance on the language you use. Again, there is a huge difference between speaking at a friend's wedding reception or giving a speech to business associates, and this section is aimed at the latter. That said it does not hurt to examine the type of vocabulary you use in any speech.

Some words can create a negative state. For example, 'actually and just', these words suggest a 'not sure' approach when used in certain sentences. Try and always use clear and concise statements that leave no room for anything other than the message. You do not want words to limit your authority, so read through your script and change any words that have a negative or unsure edge to them. You must be clear and concise because you need to impart your message in a short time period.

Try to avoid reading your speech directly from PowerPoint or cards as this only makes you look unprofessional. Use PowerPoint but, use it as a prompt to keep you on track. Nothing is more boring for your audience than someone reading the script verbatim. There are successful speakers out there who do read from cards but the more you can just use them as prompts the better. Looking directly at your audience gives you a sense of authority and confidence and your audience will naturally respect this. If you were talking to a group of friends about a subject you would be unlikely to need it all written down in front of you.

It is all about perspective.

Chapter 8: What's The Difference Between Promoting And Presenting?

As a professional speaker, I have seen two very different business models emerge in this industry – the one where the client pays you to come speak (you're a presenter) and the one where you hold your own events, fill seats yourself, and use it as an opportunity to sell something else. That's promoting.
My business model is based on clients who pay me to come speak at their event, and the message they pay for is based on my skills, my expertise, and the message their audience needs. My goal as a funny motivational speaker is to make them laugh, motivate them, teach them, and put on an amazing

show that helps them better their lives. My goal is to make my client happy, and to provide what they ask and pay for. And what they want is a speech, not a sales pitch.

My clients do not pay me to sell products and services. They do not pay me to come give a sales pitch. In fact, it is extremely frowned upon in my market. Often it is even written into the contract and agreed upon that you will not sell from the platform. There's a reason nobody wants you to do it. They don't like it. Audiences don't want a sales pitch; they want a speech. Do I have products and other services to offer? You bet. And maybe I'll mention it, or give them a flyer, or have books in the back of the room. There are subtle ways to seed instead of sell. But my goal is to fulfill the client's objective in having me come. And most of my clients will make it very clear that they are not paying me to sell.

From a personal perspective, when I'm in an audience listening to a speaker, and the speaker suddenly "tries to sell me something" it turns me off immediately, and in my eyes negates everything they have said up until that point. I tune out when the selling begins. Often this is when I will check email or run to the restroom. They have suddenly become the telemarketer on the phone who is trying to get me to buy something. Sometimes it works and I do buy. So there you go. I just don't want my selling to get in the way of their receiving my message. And people talk in this business. I don't want clients to hear that I have a reputation for selling from the platform.

But the other business model is valid. Nothing wrong with running your business that way. It's very lucrative. These people use the platform and the speech for the sole purpose of selling something. In my eyes, this is a sales pitch, no matter how you couch it. That's why this business model often depends on the speaker being responsible for gathering an audience. Many times these speakers are hosting free events, and not being paid to speak. Again – no wrong or right – just a different model. I am actually exploring this model as another stream of income. I'll let you know how it turns out. Knowing me, I'll write a book about it.

So there is the speech, and there is the sales pitch. And if your goal is to sell something, I would encourage you to write it like a speech instead of a sales pitch, with language thrown in to educate your audience about what else you have to offer and why they need it. This is called "seeding" because you are planting seeds in your program about the other things you do. There is an art to selling from the platform. We're not going to cover it here. This book is about a speech.

So what makes a speech different from a sales pitch? The intent of the speaker. The speaker's intent is to deliver a program that helps an audience fix a problem. The sales person's intent is to deliver a pitch that convinces the audience they have a problem and offers them something to buy to help them fix it.

How Do I Prepare A Speech?

Writing a good speech, if you're a professional speaker, is not easy work. But this book is for those of you who don't do this for a living – or maybe those who do, and never found an easy way to write a speech. Here's a basic speech template you can use.

Understand before you write the speech what it will be about.

Why? Because there's nothing worse

than a speaker that rambles. Speeches should be tight. You should say more with less. Know your points before you write the speech. Don't ever start a speech (or a story) without knowing where it's going to go. I think some speakers like to get up there and figure it out on the fly. There are only a handful (if that) of speakers I know who can do this well. And I'm not included.

Open in a powerful way. Why? The opening and closing moments are the two most important moments in a speech because they are remembered longest. The opening is particularly important because it sets the tone for the rest of the speech. A weak opening can lose an audience and never get them back again. I usually only need a couple of minutes with a speaker to know if I want to hear the rest. If they don't excite me right way, I'm writing a grocery list and checking my emails. It's kind of like the first chapter of a book. Make them want to read more.

Introduce yourself and establish likeability and credibility (done in the beginning and all the way through). Why? Because in order for people to believe you, listen to you, learn from you, or be impacted by you – they must like you, trust you, respect you, and believe you. Buying is emotional. And so is impacting an audience. Simply telling them what you know is not enough. You have to make this personal. Don't forget to bring your personality to the stage. I think that's one of the easiest ways to make your speech phenomenal – to bring out your personality. So many speakers don't do it. And it's a shame, because everybody has a personality.

Set up a problem that your audience acknowledges it has. Why? Because you're here to solve a problem. And if they don't understand that they have a problem, then YOU have a problem. You want your audience nodding with you, that they have a problem. A problem is something they want or need. It's usually pleasure seeking or pain avoidance. If you're a new CEO using this speech as a chance to get to know your employees and speak to them as a whole for the first time, then one of their problems might be that they don't know you or trust you – or they don't know your vision for the future of the company – or maybe they're worried that they will now lose their job. Not everybody has the same problems. You will just try and find one that many of them have, or that the client has asked you to address. For example, my messages speak to people dealing with stress and change. I know this isn't everybody, but I can't have one message for everybody. So I stick with the message I want to give (or the client asks me to give) and let it land where it lands.

Establish why you are the one to fix the problem.

Why? Again, people need to believe you. They are sitting there wondering why you should be the one to help them with this. Tell them. Sometimes this is about you showing the audience that you get what life is like where they sit, because you have experienced a similar problem or situation, and can help. Or maybe you need to show them that you have credibility in this area because you got a degree in it.

State   your   solution.

Why? You're here to fix the problem. So fix it. Give them the answer to their problem. Usually it's one big umbrella solution that requires more details. For example, my answer to dealing with stress and change is about cultivating the right perspective.

State three easy ways to get there.

Why? Because they know the answer, they just don't know how to get there.

Usually a standard speech (less than an hour) just gives three points. That's enough for an audience to handle, unless it's understood that this is going to be a training session, which is another kind of speaker and another kind of speech. I'm really focusing on the keynote speech today. If I'm speaking about dealing with stress and change, and the answer is to cultivate the right perspective, then I would give them three ways to shift their perspective.

Encourage them and Address Unspoken Objections

Why? Because an audience doesn't really care about you; they care about themselves. You are here for them. So make it about them. Think of what they might be thinking in their heads about why they can't do what you are suggesting – their objections. I know that someone in my audience who deals with stress and change is saying, "Yes, but you don't know my boss."

Give them a call to action
Why? Sometimes they don't know what to do next. Challenge them. Ask them how they will take this information and apply it in their lives. Information not acted upon is useless. Help them use it.

Q&A (Questions and Answers)
Why? Because they might have questions. And this is a good chance for you to help them even more, as they bring up issues you might not have addressed. Just don't let the Q&A get out of control. A good speaker respects his time frame. You don't have to have Q&A in your speech. Very often I don't. But if you do, don't put it last. It should never fall in the place of your power close.

Close in a powerful way
Why? Like I said earlier, this is the most powerful moment. It's what they

remember last and longest. So make it count. Put your best stuff here. Nobody likes a movie that ends poorly. Give your audience the same courtesy.

Seeding

Throughout all of this, you can make subtle mention (very subtle) of your new book, your cd, another program you offer, etc. Be very careful. If you are seen as selling from the platform, it could affect your ability to influence and tick off the client.

Chapter 9: The Voice

Voice Production

The first prerequisite of good vocal production is breathing. Even though we have been breathing all our lives, we do not necessarily do it correctly.
Many of us have a tendency to breathe from the chest. This shallow type of

breathing usually is adequate to sustain us through our daily activities. However, when we need a quick supply of oxygen while jogging or engaging in similar activities, we need to breathe in a different way. What we need to do is breathe from the chest.

Often in speech or voice classes, the student is asked to sustain an exhalation of breath for as long as possible, holding a particular note. If done correctly, this is a good exercise to determine if you are using the breathing mechanism to the best advantage. Many people cannot seem to control exhalation for longer than ten or fifteen seconds. This tells them they need to work on developing proper breathing. But the exercise also works against itself. There is often a tendency to speak or sing "from the throat" when we're running out of air. This means we're straining and thus risk losing our voices. So if you decide to try the exercise, sustain the note only until you feel your throat becoming tight and uncomfortable.

To produce sound, the vocal folds vibrate when a column of air passes through them. It's a fairly automatic process; the vocal folds adjust as we want them to. Yet if we attempt to project our voices without breathing properly, we tense our throats; we try to "squeeze" out the sound.

To relax the tension in the throat, let your jaw drop open. Produce an "ahhh" without trying to focus or project, and don't worry about how you sound. Pay attention to how you feel, and then try to carry the relaxed feeling over to other voiced sounds. Relaxed humming also is good. You should never have to force out sounds if you learn to breathe correctly.

Practice Proper Breathing

What is proper breathing for speech? Generally, it is the way we breathe when we are lying on our backs or when we are sleeping. We take in larger quantities of air, filling the abdomen and the chest, inhaling and exhaling an unobstructed flow of air. To learn to breathe in this way, lie on your back. Push as hard as you can against your abdomen with the palms of your hands. Suddenly release the pressure, and the air should flow in. Now try the same thing standing up. Keep trying till it becomes second nature to breathe deeply when you speak, especially to a group of people. The more that is required in the way of vocal projection, the more control you need to have of your breathing. In a 100-seat theatre you will not need the capacity or breath control you will in a 1,500-seat amphitheater. For an easy or relaxed sort of speech—one to entertain, for instance—you won't need the breath control you will for a more emotion-filled talk. Yet you should be able to handle any sort of speech without vocal problems.

Posture

One of the best aids to proper voice production and projection is good posture, which supports our vocal mechanism and gives it room to operate in an effective manner. You need to use your resonators to their best advantage. Resonators are those parts of the body that provide amplification for the voice, such as the tubing of a brass instrument or the sounding board of a piano. They include the throat, nose, and mouth, as well as the bones in the head and the chest. They enrich and reinforce the original tone. The more relaxed the throat, the more pleasant and full the resonation. Tension may cause undesirable voice qualities, such as whininess or breathiness. Speaking at an improper pitch also affects resonation and can tire or damage the voice.

Proper Pitch Level

To determine if you are speaking at the proper pitch level use a piano to assist in seeing how high and how low you can sing comfortably without strain. Some people, of course, will have much broader ranges than others. This doesn't matter as far as speaking is concerned. Count how many notes in your range and divide by four. A fourth of the way from the bottom should be your "habitual pitch." This means the note you hit most often in speaking. To see if that is the case, simply start to talk and sustain one of the notes rather than cutting it off. Certainly, you will not always hit the same note, nor should you try. You should be speaking within the range of this particular note, higher or lower, depending on such factors as emotional content or situation.

Just as the body needs to be relaxed and warmed up, so does the voice. Many of the relaxation exercises you learned earlier help with preparing the voice for speaking in public. A few others follow. But remember, when using your voice, always keep something in reserve. If you don't, you risk tiring yourself and straining without realizing it.

Exercises
1. Stretch the jaw as much as you can, pulling it from side to side.
2. Yawn two or three times to open up the throat.
3. Exhale as sharply as you can and then let the air rush back in.

Another aspect of voice usage is articulation, the forming of consonants using the lips, teeth, tongue, hard and soft palates, and so on. The way these are positioned, as far as contact or near contact with one another, determines the particular sound. Slight differences account for regional dialects or accents. Vast differences whether physiological or out of habit, result in unintelligible speech.

You should learn to speak clearly without emphasizing the sound so much that it calls attention to itself. This is what happened when a particular speaker kept hitting the "t" sound too hard. It came to the point where those in attendance at his speech stopped paying attention to content and concentrated only on how many times he said things like "terrific" or "transport."

Typically, people in a variety of countries, especially the United States, have sloppy speech habits. This means they are lazy about proper articulation. It's easier to pronounce a "d," rather than a "t," in words such as "better," or to say "probly" instead of "probably."

Voice Usage

Voice and speech are secondary functions of the vocal mechanism, which is primarily associated with breathing and eating. These are absolutely necessary for survival, whereas we could survive without speech, though it would probably be a very dull world.

The sounds we make with our vocal mechanisms can, so far as we know, be more exact and varied than those of other life forms. Even so, we make many nonverbal sounds, those that can communicate though not through the symbols we call words. We cry, wail, hum, grunt, or scream, and the variety within each of these types of sounds can have any number of meanings, from rage to purring contentment.

Even when we use words themselves, the manner in which we say them varies greatly, with any number of implied meanings. Spoken with a tremor, the sentence, "Your brother is coming home," could suggest fear. Said another way it could suggest excitement or dread or happiness.

Delivered with a sharp staccato tone, it could show disgust or anger. The manner of delivery, the nonverbal message of the sound, often carries as much or more weight in communicating meaning as do the words themselves.

Yet these nonverbal aspects are inexact. We've all experienced misunderstanding in the communication process. A large percentage of the time this is because the subtext, the nonverbal part of the communication process comes across more loudly than the intended message. Thus a listener mishears the words themselves.

The four aspects of voice usage are timing, volume, pitch, and quality. Timing can be further broken down into rate, duration, pause, and rhythm.

Timing

Rate refers to the overall speed with which a speech is delivered and can be measured by the number of words uttered per minute. Rate is determined by the emotional content of the words. A sad or reflective speech would be delivered much more slowly than would one filled with excitement. A complicated speech would be delivered at a slower rate than would something that is easy to follow and to understand. Duration refers to the length of each individual sound, and, like rate, is dependent on the emotional effects desired and on the importance of the individual words. For example, if you were going to build suspense and an atmosphere of fear and apprehension, the rate would be faster than for a piece where the effect of each word is important.

Duration is also a means of emphasis, of highlighting a certain point. "You w-i-l-l-

I-I be here at two o'clock sharp." "I said right n-o-o-o-w!"

The effect of a word or phrase can be heightened or pointed up by yet another device, pausing. If those giving speeches pause before a word, they are telling the audience to pay close attention because they are about to make an important point. Comedians often pause before a punch line.

Pauses also provide oral punctuation. It would be difficult for an audience to comprehend a selection that was read at an even rate. On the other hand, you should not pause every time there is written punctuation. If you do, the speech will be choppy.

You can also use pauses to determine phrasing, which varies from one situation to another and also depends on emotional and logical content.

The last aspect of timing is rhythm. Rhythm, even in prose, involves the recurrence of a word, an idea, a sound, or a pattern of sounds. It can be found in such easily spotted devices as alliteration, but more often exists in the flow of the language. For instance, compare Martin Luther King's "I Have a Dream" speech to Abraham Lincoln's Gettysburg address. Both have a particular rhythm, but they are much different from each other.

Volume

Volume is determined somewhat by the mood and the size of the audience. You'd mostly convey anger more loudly, that is at a higher decibel level, than would serenity. Like pauses, volume can be used to point up or to emphasize. For example, the words that should be spoken louder in the following are italicized: What are you doing here? Can't you mind your own business?

Pitch

An effective way of communicating meaning is pitch, or changes in the frequency of sound. When a sound is spoken at a higher pitch level than other words in a phrase, it calls attention to itself. Go back to the example at the end of the last paragraph. Try to say the words in the two sentences at the same pitch level using only an increase in volume for emphasis. Now try to say the same two sentences by increasing the volume and raising the pitch level of the italicized words. Changes in pitch not only occur from word to word, but within individual words. The latter, of course, is called inflection. A rising inflection can convey a question, a sense of doubt, or a sense of disbelief or shock. A falling inflection often conveys determination or certainty.

Quality

Quality, the remaining aspect of voice, refers to the changes in the overtones in one's voice when speaking Changes in quality can be used to indicate changes in meaning, or to portray emotions. Quality is most often associated with mood and feeling. For example, a gruff or husky quality may indicate an intense depth of feeling, such as sorrow, whereas a whining quality is often associated with pleading.

Chapter 10: Best Ted Talk

Now when we have discussed a lot about the essence of communication and its prerequisites, we will divert towards some practical examples of TED speakers. These speakers have been pointed out to have exclusive speaking powers and classy gestures which make them stand out in many with remarkable qualities. Although there are a lot of other names, but due to the restriction of the space we will mention a few.

The main aim is to formulate the attention to, read about these spectacular TED speakers, and point puts some distinctive properties possessed by their presentation sessions. We will then thrash out some familiar uniqueness and qualities, which when followed can help the individuals in becoming the attractive TED talkers over the globe.

1) **Pranav Mistry.** At TEDIndia, Pranav Mistry has a brilliant demonstration on several apparatus that lend a hand to the physical world intermingle with the huge arena of data — including a thorough gaze at his Sixth-Sense apparatus and a new, concentration-changing phenomenon "laptop." In the live query session, he explored much more.

2) **Tony Robbins** is another remarkable speaker in the TED world where he talks about the invisible forces, the blueprint of their amalgamation and the effect of these forces on the day to day activities of individuals and societies.

3) **David Gallo** is also an attention gathering speaker. On one of the recent sessions, he equipped his presentation with a multi perspective footage which was all embellished with the classy and colorful scenes of the ocean world. The video recording has an elevated

resolution with lobby group of cuttlefish, octopus and neon lights sprinkled all around. This short talk was designed to pay tribute to the exclusive work of ocean explorers like Roger Hanlon and Edith Widder.

4) **Dan Gilbert**, author of a number of masterpieces, has offered an exigent claim that if all the needs are fulfilled, happiness is eternal. He claims that possessing the material things is not the only key to success and happiness. He talks about the importance of balances and check points for psychological disasters.

5) **Susan Cain** has also gained remarkable attention because of her challenging and exclusive ideas. When all and sundry utter out the efficacy of being extrovert Susan demonstrates that being an introvert is an unparalleled power. She passionately claims that the hidden talents and the unique set of abilities possessed by

introverts must be improved and celebrated.

Although the list is quite long and full yet, we have mentioned some most discussed characters in the TED talks. Now we will give a brief narrative for some characteristics possessed by theses speakers.

This not some formula that will give out the same formulaic answer every time, yet it will serve as the major route map of the field. You have to polish the expertise till the level of your brilliant audience. The audience is now very informative as well as critical. You cannot deny their talent, so you have to be alert and conscious about their demands.

Major commonalities among the top TED talkers

Confident body language

The major reason for discussing the high profile TED Talks was to check and elaborate some major points which can help the speakers in the replenishment of their speaking skills. And if you look at the visuals you can easily spot the marvelous body language and gestures posed by these speakers.

The self-belief assures that the speaker has firm beliefs on what he is talking or delivering to the consultation. So sooner than you are organized for your new venture, get a confident body language.

Grip over the idea

Another striking similarity between all the remarkable TED talkers is their grip over the idea so that they are thinking of experts on the particular topic. Grip and grasp do not mean that the speaker gets all the knowledge about the topic; in fact it states that the choice of subject matter is so professional and exclusive that the facts are considered understandable.

It is necessary that the speaker is ready for all types of questions and queries, which add to his confidence and professional approach. So start preparing efficiently

Challenging ideas

If you look at the profile of the speakers provided above or you search it yourself, you can easily distinguish the worth of challenging ideas. The audience is ready to admit the ideas and facts which are usually counter striking and parallel to the already held facts and beliefs. Challenging doesn't mean that you start challenging genuine facts and figures. The task of creating and polishing challenging ideas must be performed with care, so that no further debate can be elaborated after the TED talk finishes.

Challenging ideas are given a new dimension of thinking and pondering, so this new direction must be firm.

One step ahead

If you have planned to start or initiate your talk on some already known fact, then the most accurate and effective approach will be to move one step ahead in thinking and approaching the facts. Add some extra knowledge of the beliefs of the audience so that there is some center of attraction for discussing the already known idea or belief.

It may require extensive research work from the speaker before he presents his talks to the audience. But when formerly the milieu is well prepared, it will bring extra strength for the TED talk and the whole session of conversation.

Enigmatic approach

Another common feature of all well know TED speakers is their ability to provide a complete charismatic package for the whole TED talk.

Whether it includes the subject matter or the gestures of the encoder, everything is equally crucial for the success of the session. It demands an additive approach. It infers that every minute item adds more and more power to the TED talk if all items are taken care of.

Never rely on one or few strengths of your speaking style. Make yourself a complete package of success and rigor, so that you can be considered as a guru in TED talks.

Chapter 11: Believe In Yourself

Anxiety has become one of the leading root causes of several mental health problems. The vicious cycle normally involves low level fears. When you over worry, you create low level anxiety, which then triggers more anxious thoughts that can lead to panic. Once you are caught in that vicious cycle, the other negative emotions start to creep in: frustration, depression, and even anger. The best way for you to get out of this vicious cycle is to start feeling better about yourself. When you start by learning how to believe in the new behaviour that your after, you will find it easier to overcome your panic and all the negative emotions that come with it.

What is self-belief? It is the way you see yourself as a whole or in a situation like public speaking. It is the opinion you have of yourself. The thoughts you have about public speaking. They say that you are what you believe you are. With low self-beliefs come negative thoughts about yourself in one or more areas of your life. Your focus is on all your shortcomings and weaknesses, like if you imagine yourself speaking in public all you see is an image, or you hear yourself falling apart. When you have low self-belief, you can lead on to experiencing different kinds of mental health issues such as phobias, anxiety, panic, which is essentially high level fear or anxiety, or even eating disorders, and depression.

Self-beliefs are normally linked to a person's temperament. But your negative experiences as a child can also make you think bad of yourself. People who have been neglected or abused as a child normally have low self-confidence. Others have experienced social exclusions, poor physical health, and bullying trauma. They tend to worry about things in there lives because they feel like they cannot match up to other people's expectations.

Low self-belief that leads to panic whilst speaking can have create problems in other areas of your life like your personal relationships. It can affect your career and social life as well. This is why it is vital that you make it a priority to do something about your belief system so that you can increase your chances of overcoming your panic. Here are some helpful techniques you can use in boosting your self beliefs:

•You will only be able to change the panic you feel when speaking publicly, if you change the negative beliefs about yourself when visualising your future speaking engagements, when you have a clear understanding and solidify your new beliefs you have completed step one. So try with thinking about the all the weaknesses that you see in yourself. When did you start thinking and feeling like this? Can you pinpoint any situation or event that could have triggered that those thoughts of panic?

•After you have gained a better understanding of your negative beliefs and the exact moment you trigger these thoughts, whether its an image, a sound or a feeling, or a combination of these, the next step is to start gathering evidences that can challenge your beliefs. Take the time to write those evidences so you can refer to them when you start feeling anxious or panicky. For instance, if you think that your heart rate goes up as soon as you see an image in your head, or you hear a certain sound or word, write it down and start evidencing your thought patterns and triggers so you have a clear understanding of what beliefs you need to change.

•Here are a couple of positive thinking exercises that you can do:

Jot down the strengths you think you have and the other things that you appreciate in yourself. What do you think are your best skills or talents ? Do you like to talk to people? Do you like being in a group situation with friends? Do you have a flexible attitude? You can also add your personal achievements and skills that you have. Have you done nice things to other people that they appreciated? Are you good at dancing or drawing? This is your private moment, so do not feel shy in writing all the positive things about you. This list will be very helpful for you during those days when you feel anxious or worried about a engagement coming up.

Talk with people who love and support you. You don't need to suffer the company of people who make you feel worse about yourself. Even if it is your own family, if they are not bringing positive things in your life right now, it is best to spend your time away from them. When you are feeling better and stronger, you can then spend some time with them. But make it your priority to spend more time with those who make you see life in a more positive way.

oStart taking up a new hobby that can have positive effects in your life. Have you always wanted to learn how to cook or to knit? Don't put it off.

oSet positive goals that can make you feel inspired. Perhaps you can start training for a 10k run, or maybe you can redecorate your home. The key is to have a full life so it contributes to squeezing out any negative thoughts about panic.

Chapter 12: The 30% Rule

We've all seen it the infomercial on TV; the overzealous in-store demonstrator, or the conference presenter who acts like he has had ten cups of coffee; that presenter who yells out "ARE YOU READY!", and even though you yell a reply they keep saying "I can't hear you!".

If you are anything like me, it makes your skin crawl. It feels so unnatural and inauthentic that you can see the audience turning off before anything has even begun. On the other end of the spectrum, you see these speakers who give off a similar high energy vibe but have the audience eating out of their hands.

You've seen it on the TV, or in movies like Jordan Belfort on "The Wolf of Wall Street" motivating, chanting, and almost hypnotising his staff each day; or

Ellen DeGeneres dancing and fist pumping on TV every day.

I've been to Tony Robbin's "Unleash the Power Within" and seen the high energy, powering voice, and personal style he brings. The way he transforms a room of over five thousand people into a sober nightclub of personal development is amazing.

Fists pumping, jumping up and down dancing, tears, laughter, and lifetime changes occurring.

The thing you need to understand about all these great speakers is that they are bringing their own style to the stage. We need to stop comparing ourselves to them, as they weren't always anywhere near the finished product you see today. As soon as you start to try and mimic anyone, you turn from a speaker to an actor.

You will lose your biggest asset... you! The message you are trying to send will no longer be authentic and let me tell you this; it's hard work trying to pull off something that you aren't.

Many of my students have told themselves a story and created a limiting belief because of these great speakers. They tell themselves "why even bother if it's not going to be as good as them?".

Remind yourself that you have a message to share; a chance to be the change you want to see in the world. You have a framework now to implement, and the more you do it, the more rapid your improvement and impact will be.

Applying the 30% rule; it's simple.

Take you normal likeable self and add 30% to everything. Your volume, your facial expressions, hand gestures, and body language.

Playing small with all of those feels safe but looks scared. You must create your own energy and make it contagious with your audience. The speaker who stands on stage with their hands by their side, or jumps on camera using the same tone of voice they do when talking to a friend at the end of a long day; or the person whose facial expression look like they have modelled Sylvester Stallone (who suffers from facial nerve palsy); that speaker, no matter how interesting their content is, will struggle to have maximum impact.

Adding 30% onto everything allows you to stay yourself, but keep the entire audience engaged. I suggest putting some of these into your day to day interactions and see what you notice. It's not often that people will have a negative reaction to you if you add some extra arm movements, enthusiastically greet people, smile or laugh a little more, and use your voice to express your stories and message.

There are a few areas you can focus on initially to incorporate in daily life, which will help:

- Use your hands. Stop keeping them in your pocket or by your side. Channel your inner Italian and use nice wide hand movements.
- Smile, frown, and nod show people that you are interested in what you are telling them or are at least being receptive to what they are sharing with you.
- Stand tall, shoulders back.
- Speak 30% less
- Learn to control your breathing to manage your voice

The first three points are just a matter of you being more self-aware, watching recordings of yourself, and being critical. The other two points require a bit more explanation.

Speaking less to achieve more is a counterintuitive idea. As speakers, we have this worry whenever there is a quiet space. We desperately want to fill it. Unfortunately, we do this with umm's, ahhh's, and's and so's.

One or two of these in a speech isn't the end of the world, as it is something we often do that every day in conversation as well; but one or two in every sentence will kill the whole talk.

How can you stop yourself doing that?

First, let's understand why we do them so much in presentations and not in conversations.

To me, they are like the verbal full stop for a lot of people.

We get to the end of a sentence. Often, we do know what we are going to say next, but to make sure there is no silence we just insert one of the above words.

One part of the solution, which I would encourage you to work on, is pausing! A pause while speaking feels like an eternity but is just what your audience needs to digest the information you just shared.

A speaker who doesn't pause isn't an expert in their industry. They speak quickly to make sure you don't have time to process what they are saying logically. Think of the stereotypical used car salesmen as they fire away a million things at you. I compare this to the best sales people I know who live by the mantra 'he who speaks most loses'.

Record a short talk at home and have a look at when and how often you say 'umm', 'ahh', 'so', or 'and'. You will quickly see it is when you are transitioning onto a new point, or at the end/beginning of a sentence.

Better yet, if you are feeling game, join my free community on Facebook called "Speaker Nation: Become a powerful fearless speaker". Join now and post a welcome video with a bit about what you do. If you like, I will even give you some feedback on it!

I've nicknamed the next skill the "Invisible Improvement".

It's one of those aspects that the audience won't be able to pick up what you have changed in your presentation style, but they will notice and comment about it.

This is your breathing; something we take for granted, as on average we do it 20k - 30k times each day without even thinking about it. Here's the thing though; when it comes to public speaking, we need to breathe differently. The method the top speakers use is called the 'Diaphragmatic Breathing Technique'.

Our natural tendency is to breathe in and out of our chest. The result is less oxygen into our lungs and running out of air towards the end of a sentence; but as we run short on air our voice tends to trail off. It's like our excitement wains as the sentence progresses.

This leads to our voice becoming softer, tone, pitch, and inflection are non-existent. Worst of all is we get short of breath and start taking shorter shallower breaths.

Diaphragmatic breathing will take some focus to become a habit but will allow you to speak louder, have a consistent tone, and be able to easily modify your inflection at the appropriate time. When we naturally breathe, we draw our stomach in and expand our chest.

What you need to practice is creating a bulge out of your stomach as your inhale and allow your stomach to come in as your breath out and speak. This engages our diaphragm which is the strongest muscle we can use to help with breathing and speaking.

Incorporating this technique into your speaking style will also naturally slow you down, as you must breathe in at some stage. There are certain cues to breathe in. Anywhere that a comma would go if you were to write what you were saying down, or any full stop is a perfect time to take a breath.

Changing your breathing will lead you to pause more. More pausing will lead to a slower talk, and a slower talk will lead to more of your overarching message being absorbed. Fancy that!

AND a good dose of oxygen is what keeps the mind focused… Ever wondered why they make you blow into a paper bag when having a panic attack? It's to bring focus to the breath, which helps calm the mind, which then helps curb your fight or flight response.

Wake up every morning and focus on one minute of speaking using this new technique. The more comfortable you can get with it in non-stressful environments, the easier the transition will be, come presentation time.

Chapter 13: List Of Benefits Derived From Public Speaking

Delivering a speech in front of many people is a phobia experienced by many. A lot of people prefer touching spiders or be trapped in a confined space rather than be tasked to stand in front an audience of thousands to deliver a speech. Public speaking is often perceived as something really risky – others faint while doing so because of pressure and intimidation. Many people tend to feel insecure and fearful of standing on the podium because one or more of the following possibilities: (1) they might suddenly freeze up; (2) they might forget what they will say; (3) their audience might get bored with the speech; (4) the audience might walk out; and (5) the audience might ask questions that are difficult to answer.

Public speaking is often perceived as a major source of stress. But perhaps, you are already very familiar with the sayings, "No risk no reward" and "No pain, no gain." The same is true in this situation. You will never be able to build your confidence fully if you will constantly veer away from the crowd. Once you gather the strength and the courage to face a big audience, you will be delighted because it is a very enlightening and empowering experience. Public speaking can be scary at first, but it does not mean that you won't be successful at it.

Here's the trick. In order to convince yourself to give public speaking a try, instead of looking at the fearful and intimidating things about it, you should look at the benefits instead. In this chapter, you will know what rewards await those who are courageous enough to step into the podium.

Public Speaking Benefit #1: Hone your critical thinking skills

A great way to build your skills in critical thinking is by practicing public speaking. The process of crafting the message and writing the actual speech to be delivered requires a high level of critical thinking. You should analyze your audience and try to profile them so that you can come up with convincing arguments that will successfully persuade them to take your side. Also, you need to outline points that will logically flow towards your intended conclusion. Choosing evidence to be presented is also a challenge because you would only prefer relevant points to be included in your speech.

Public Speaking Benefit #2: Develop and grow personally and professionally

Success in the personal and the professional realms require excellent skills in communication. If you are well-versed in speaking in front of many people, chances are, you are a great communicator. Most likely, you are familiar with the effective methods of communicating points. Remember, all significant relationships are built by communication.

Public Speaking Benefit #3: Successfully create useful and important social connections

Public speaking paves the way towards instant connections to important people. This is one of the most established and time-tested methods of creating social connections and network. Every time you deliver a speech well, there is a high possibility for you to get noticed. You will be surprised one day to find a VIP quoting things that you have said in one of your speeches.

To maximize all the possible connections, you can try accommodating conversations even after the speech. Socialize with people after your talk. If possible, mingle with your audience. Let them see your human side. Allow them to appreciate you inside and out.

Public Speaking Benefit #4: Overcome all of your fears

Public speaking is the most feared thing according to a recent study, and it is closely followed by death. Yes, it is that intimidating. But hey, if you succeed in this field, just imagine what other big fears you can conquer.

Public Speaking Benefit #5: Boost your self-confidence and self-esteem

The ultimate self-confidence builder and self-esteem booster is public speaking. On top of that, public speaking serves as an instrument for fighting off any kind of insecurities and anxieties. When you get the hang of public speaking, it can be very empowering. In the long run, you will have the confidence to express what you have in mind.

Public Speaking Benefit #6: Advance professionally

The capability to speak in front of a large audience can help you attain professional advancement. Among the specific examples are the following:

1.You will be able to impress your boss. Bosses favor people who can do public speaking because it is an indicator that the person has the following characteristics: professionalism, poise, abilities in leadership, critical thinking, and creativity.

2. You will successfully gain publicity. When you know how to speak in front of an audience, you can put your message across faster.

3. You will be able to define your public persona. When you already have the public persona, it will be much easier to communicate with your audience.

4. You will be able to develop eloquence.

5. You will have the unique privilege to affect change.

Chapter 14: Public Speaking Vs. Conversation

Come to think about it, what is the difference between public speaking and talking? Have you ever thought about it? Public speaking is pretty much talking, the only difference is that you have a bigger audience.

Did you know that public speaking and talking are so similar that it becomes easier for you to slip in a slight public speech into an everyday conversation? You can do it so well that the person you are speaking to might not even be able to notice the difference.

This is all about practice. No one wakes up one day and becomes a good public speaker from nowhere. Everyone starts from somewhere, and as long as you are willing to give it a try, there is every possibility that you will be able to build up on the little that you have and in the long run perfect your art.

The concept of public speaking and having a conversation is similar, with the only difference being that in public speaking nothing is private, and there is an ultimate goal. Having a conversation can at times be just about making small talk and getting to pass time, but with public speeches, there is always an objective; passing some information, sharing some knowledge and so forth. The most important thing about public speaking is the call to action.

With public speaking there is always something in your mind that you want the listener to do, something you want them to feel, a message you want them to get; in most cases you already have an outcome in your mind, an outcome that is desirable to your immediate cause. Having a normal conversation on the other hand can be open-ended. It might be possible that you have a general goal, but you might not necessarily be trying to convince your friends to do something as is the case with public speaking.

It is easier for you to hone your skills in public speaking by becoming more interactive with your daily conversations as you get to build up your confidence. The following are some simple pointers that can help you set the ball rolling:

- **Plan** – Always plan what you are going to say in the speech ahead of time. This will help you be preemptive and be ready for anything that might come out of your schedule

- **Practice** – Always practice saying what you are going to say in advance, so that you can make sure it feels and sounds right in your mind before you say it out to the audience
- **Clarity of speech** – Speaking clearly is always a prerequisite to perfecting your act in public speaking, because it makes it easier for you to be heard.
- **Confidence** – Always be sure to exude a sense of confidence while you are speaking. Speak slowly and authoritatively

When you are delivering the speech, be sure to be on the lookout for the reaction of the audience. You need to know whether or not you are able to persuade them. Remember that the audience will probably not know that you are taking a keen interest in their reactions, so this gives you an upper hand.

Chapter 15: How To Deliver Short Notice Or Impromptu Speech

There are four problems that new public speakers feel exist with short notice speeches.

The first is fear of facing the audience.

This is a non-event. The audience want the speaker to succeed. Also, it is important to stress to speakers that they make short notice speeches in everyday conversations, every day.

The second is a memory lapse.

This should not be a problem because no one knows what the speaker is going to say. Using a personal experience can overcome this, too.

The third is the fear of going blank as you are about to start.

The speaker must learn to focus on a word that enshrines the introduction as they approach the podium.

The fourth fear is not having enough material.

The speaker needs only one point to develop so really it is not an issue.

Now, let us get onto the actual presentation of the speech.

Remember it is a speech. It must contain an opening, a body and a conclusion.

The opening must be designed to involve your audience and be no longer than thirty seconds in a three minute speech. Slow down your opening to allow the audience to get on board.

The body is two minutes long. Here you make your main point and give evidence to support that point. Keep the pace slow to allow your listeners to understand your argument/points. It also gives you time for more thought.

Use all the speech tricks you can, e.g. body language, gesture, variations in volume and the speed of your voice to create your 'picture'.

Your conclusion needs only thirty seconds. Remind the audience strongly of your message in a dramatic and emotional way.

There are a few other tricks that speakers can use if they feel that they have limited material. They are:

When the speaker is called to give their speech, they should move slowly from their place to the podium. This allows them to marshal their thoughts, especially about their opening.

Before they start they must stand comfortably, take a deep breath and look around at their audience making eye contact before they begin.

They must speak slowly allows themselves time to think. It shortens the speech content and allows the subconscious to work ahead of their spoken words.

Palm card notes should only contain one word per idea to jog their memory.

if they lack enough material, then they must concentrate on giving the best delivery possible.

One final point: Timing is important but it is not the 'be all and end all'. Remember the speaker must be encouraged to say what they want to say and sit down. Remind them that the motto of good speakers is, "Stand up, speak up and shut up."

Chapter 16: Practicing Nonverbals

Tori McDermott

Topic: Nonverbal communication

Learning Objectives: After completing this learning activity, students will be able to:

Demonstrate effective use of nonverbals

Description of Assignment/Activity: This activity is designed to help students gain confidence with their use of expressive nonverbals by acting out famous nonverbal scenes.

Materials needed: None

Prep time: 5 minutes (if you come up with scenes prepped for the class)

Assignment time: 15-20 minutes

Instructions for Instructor:

Review with students the importance of effective use of nonverbal communication and techniques for developing effective nonverbals.

Break the students into pairs.

Have each pair take 5-7 minutes to brainstorm a famous nonverbal scene from a movie or come up with a scene that can be conveyed nonverbally. It might be good to have a pocket list of scenes if your students are having trouble coming up with an idea for the nonverbals or allow them to use electronic devices to search for topics. Some examples might be acting out a fast food drive through or finding out some sort of shocking information.

Each pair of students will present their scene to the class without any verbal communication.

The class has 2 minutes to guess what is going on in the scene. The class must also guess if the scene is from a tv show or movie.

Debrief with the class about the effectiveness of some nonverbal signals over others.

Instructions for Students:

Get into groups of two.

Each group needs to convey a 1-minute scene to the class using nonverbals only. Words or sounds are not allowed. You are allowed to act out famous movie scenes or create your own scene.

Before we start presenting, at the end of each scene the class will guess what the group is trying to convey to the audience and how effective the nonverbal communication strategies were at conveying the intended emotion.

After the entire class has presented, as a class, we will recap what makes for effective use of nonverbals?

Necessary Background: This requires a background on the importance of expressiveness and nonverbals in speeches. The students should have some type of knowledge about effect expressive and nonverbal communication techniques.

Special considerations: Students may have trouble coming up with a scene, so

143

have a few scenes to give out for groups that cannot come up with a scene on their own. But try to encourage students to be creative. If they own the scene, they will be more connected and engaged.

Debrief: After the first activity, be sure to debrief about the nonverbals that people were able to easily recognize and the ones that were cloudy. Ask your students to identify the techniques they used to enhance understanding with their nonverbal.

Variations:

Instead of letting the students pick the scene, you can assign them a specific scene.

You can scale this activity up and add more students into the groups to make the scenes more complex.

Trouble spots:

Make sure to set ground rules for the class about what is appropriate (no sexually explicit scenes, etc.)

Make sure to rule out certain scene possibilities (ex: anything with death, guns, rape as this may be a trigger for some students)

Students may feel a high level of communication anxiety not being allowed to use verbal communication. Stress this is a learning activity with no right or wrong answers.

Chapter 17: Derive Some Inspiration

Communication is an art; a skill that can be acquired and practiced to perfection. Theoretical knowledge, techniques and tips are good ways to master this skill but a more important method is learning by examples. Examples set by others can help you in understanding better. For example, when you are audience to a certain speaker, you will be able to make connections better. You will relate better to the reactions of the audience to different aspects of the presentation.

Here are some of the big names that have made mastered not only the art of communicating but also making a connection to ensure that the audience is completely hooked to every word they say because for them, the art of communication probably determines the fate of their career as does yours.

1. **Michelle Obama:** The first lady of the USA is an excellent communicator. She speaks to influence, whether with her passion or with her personal stories, she finds a connection with her audience and makes her point in the best way possible. Her presence and clarity of message coupled with her composure makes her a great communicator. Some of the other attributes you should notice when this lady speaks is her body language – eye contact, the energy and emotions she brings into her speech touch the audience she is targeting.

2. **Marco Rubio**: He has been a senator for a couple of months, but the excellent public speaker has been mentioned more than once because of his confidence and authenticity which impresses his audience. A clear, to the point message with a personal touch is just the right ingredients for not only

effective communication but also impressive. Marco Rubio is just not a great speaker but also applauded for capturing the interest of his audience through his writing; a memoir – An American Son.

3. **Melissa Franklin:** The 21 year old four-time Olympic Gold medalist is just not the amazing swimmer we know her for, but also a great communicator. Her confidence at an age of seventeen is remarkable and rarely seen. A poolside interview after her win in the 100m backstroke, her emotions touched the audience when she said how important it was that her parents witness her victory. Emotions cannot be faked; the audience can always differentiate between fake and genuine. She will easily become the role models of many aspiring young ones out there.

4. **Ryan Seacrest:** Though you might think that it is his looks and wits that make him popular, which might even be true to some extent, but it his energy and enthusiasm that keeps all eyes and ears hooked to him. The openness with which he delivers creates likeability, a connection with his audience. Focus on his voice, the modulation, the feel of energy in it and a touch of personal feel makes him popular among his audience.

5. **Cory Booker:** The former mayor of Newark, and the current US junior senator from New Jersey, says it all with his smiles. The excitement and energy he radiates are infectious as he speaks to his audience. Humor, emotions and a personal touch are the secret ingredients of Booker. Empathy and connection with the audience are two important components Booker exhibits in his communications. He also

makes sure to keep his message crisp and clear, so that he doesn't bore the people listening to him.

6. **Sheryl Sandberg:** The COO of Facebook, Sandberg was featured in Time 100, the annual list of the 100 most influential people in the World according to Time magazine. It is not an overstatement when she is said to be an excellent communicator. She keeps her audience in mind, and so when she gives Tech talks, she breaks it down for her audience with analogies and stories they can relate to. The encoding and relaying is makes it certain that the decoding is invariably accurate and enjoyable; and this makes her a very effective communicator.

7. **Bill Clinton**: The envy of speakers across the globe is how he has been named by many. A one of his kind speaker, President Clinton is known for

improvising his prepared speech. More than once he had put aside his rehearsed speech and spoken from his heart to capture his audience. The effect he has on his audience can easily rally them and convince even those who had not decided which side to take. He proves to be a role model for speakers of all ages and across all genres.

8. **Steven Colbert & John Stewart:** The pair of them takes communication to a new level altogether. Humor is a strong component to add in your communication but you have to get it right or it can prove to be disastrous. Who better to learn from than this pair? They aim to simplify the inner workings of political procedures which includes the complicated policies on campaign financing and other related topics. The energetic and witty comedy experts come to the audiences' level to

connect with them and make them popular among the audience.

9. **Jack Dorsey**: The co-founder and CEO of twitter as well as the founder and CEO of Square, Wall Street Journal gave him the award of "Innovator of the Year Award". Simplifying the complex is said to be his specialty. Speaking in a simple but precise way to reach his audience is what makes him an effective communicator. He artfully uses stories and analogies to cater for the better understanding of his audience and that is how he keeps them hooked to his words. His easy movement on stage and gestures and visual aids keeps his audience engaged – very important to note.

10. **Marissa Mayer:** Former spokesperson for Google and the current CEO of yahoo is known for her smile intellect and great communication skill. Her

passion and determination in her work has set an example for others to follow and these attributes filters down to her speech when she interacts with the audience. A clear and to the point but simple messages gives her the most desirous of results and that is what people notice in a successful person – the results you are able to get.

These were some of the great example setters who have excelled in the field of communication and public speaking. You will realize there are some common attributes you can recall and we will discuss this in a latter chapter of this book.

Meanwhile, while these names are still fresh in your mind, why don't you do a quick search on YouTube and watch a couple of these people in action? This will give you a firsthand experience as an audience. How you feel as the speakers exihibit the different attributes I had highlighted above.

Chapter 18: The Role Of The Audience In Successful Public Speaking

The three main components of any public speaking process are:

1. The Audience
2. The Speaker
3. The Message

In this chapter, we shall be considering the audience component of a public speaking process. The audience in this context refers to the people to who a presentation is made in the public speaking process.

Know Your Audience before Speaking to a Group

Your goal in speaking to a group is to inform, persuade, or entertain them. To achieve any or all of those objectives, you should know their interests, likes, and dislikes. Before you speak to a group of people, you should learn as much about them and their interests as possible. You can also find information about them and their mood at the beginning and during your speech. You can then tailor your speech to their needs, and better ensure a positive reaction from them.

Questions you may have include:

i. Why should you find out about the audience?

ii. How can you find out about the audience?

Why You Need To Know Your Audience

Your purpose in speaking to a group is to inform, persuade, or entertain the audience. Your motivation is to get satisfaction from expressing your ideas and getting recognition or applause from the audience.

In order to achieve your purpose, as well as to get the expression and applause you desire, you must satisfy the audience with something in which they are interested. Thus, it is important to know what your audience is interested in, what their expectations are and even what mood they are in.

How to Find Out About the Audience

You can find out about the audience through research before you speak, through interaction at the beginning of your talk, and by making adjustments during the speech.

Before you speak, and even before you prepare your speech, you should know what sort of audience you would have. What is the nature of the group? What do they expect to hear from you? Do they have any special interests or prejudices about which you should be aware?

Who Is In The Audience?

In speaking to a group of managers at work, you have a good idea of who will be in the audience. There may be some individuals to be cautious of or to whom you should focus the speech. For example, I knew an Air Force Major who would always direct his speech to the highest-ranking officer in the audience. He knew who was important to his career in giving his presentations.

If you find out about some key people in the audience, you can use them in your opening comments to gain rapport with the audience. Everyone likes a humorous comment about the boss, at your expense, not at his or hers. Now, that is very important note though.

At the Beginning of the Talk

Comments you make at the beginning of the speech or presentation can give you clues about your audience and their expectations.

Comedian tested audience:

Old-time comedian Milton Berle would start off his comedy routines before large audiences by telling five different types of one-liner jokes. From the reaction he got from the jokes, he would know if the majority of the audience was in the mood for silly humour, political humour, or blue jokes. Berle had an encyclopaedic mind for jokes and comedy routines, so he would then present the routine that was effective for the particular audience that night.

Prepare for Some Modifications

Although, you cannot be expected to have several versions of a speech or presentation, you can use some opening remarks and responses from the audience to give you an idea or a clue to the direction of their interest and perhaps their mood. If the audience seems in a light mood, perhaps you could sprinkle in a few jokes to keep their interest. If they seemed to be very serious about your topic, you could get right to the meat of the matter.

Do not be a Self-Centred Speaker

Nothing is worse than going to a speech, wanting to hear some information, and having the speaker drone on and on about something of no interest to you or most of the audience. The speaker must get an idea in the beginning of his talk concerning what the audience wants, not what he or she wants to say.

During the Talk

While you are giving a talk, you can often tell if the audience is enthralled with your material or if they are getting bored or restless. The problem usually occurs when the speaker is so caught up in what he or she is saying that the audience might as well not be there. In a humorous talk, the speaker can usually tell if things aren't going good if there is silence and the audience is not laughing at the jokes. Some humorous speakers will blame the audience and say, "What's wrong with you people? This is funny material." May be it is funny to him, but apparently, it is not to this audience.

In any situation where it seems that the audience is getting restless or bored, the best thing to do is to summarize things and to end your talk. It is better to have a shorter speech than to go too long and bore people. This is true in any speech. As a preacher and a teacher, there are times I prepare to deliver a sermon with five key points but upon looking at the mood and response of the congregation, I end up with three of those points and stop.

The Benefit of Knowing the Audience

When you know what the audience wants and likes, when you know what mood the audience is in, and when you know something about the audience, they become more interested in what you have to say.

Often the speaker does not even have to be a good speaker, and sometimes the subject does not have to be very good, but if the audience feels there is good communication, they will listen and enjoy the speech. They will also give good recognition and applause for the effort. Knowing the audience can result in the benefits you want from giving the talk.

A. Audience Analysis

i. Determine Demographic, Psychographic And Situational Characteristics of Your Audience

Just as a gardener must tend to the individual needs of each plant, a speaker must know his/her audience well. Learn all that you can about your audience in order to meet the needs of your speaking occasion.

You may need to consider the following;

· Age
· Gender
· Education

- Occupation
- Language
- Audience Size
- Social Status
- Audience Knowledge of Subject
- Audience Interests and Needs
- Audience Perceptions

Size: How many people will show up? Is the group to be large or small? A single person or a banquet hall's worth of folk? Formality and structure work well for presentations to big groups, but in small settings they may seem stifling, thus a more casual approach is usually preferable. It will naturally be harder to make a large audience feel involved in your presentation than a small one; however, you can figure out ways to encourage participation in both.

Demographics: Who will be listening? Age, career, ethnic, or cultural background, socioeconomic status, educational background, gender - they all play a role in what you can and should say to your audience. You will address a room of middle-aged female accountants from Germany differently than you would a bunch of college-age male musicians from Alabama. Deference plays well with old people, occupational expertise with wage earners, and a dash of commiseration with the young. Consider what to exclude as much as what to include. If the people who came to hear your financial advice don't own stocks, they'll tune out when you start talking about reductions in the dividend tax.

Knowledge level: What do they already know about this subject? Are you chatting with balloon technology experts about new developments in the field, or are you introducing the topic to non-professionals? Whether you are informing or persuading, before you can jump in to the heart of your subject, you may need to prep the audience with some background and history.

Motivation: What do your listeners hope to get out of your presentation? Your biggest concern in this area: Are they paying to hear you speak? If they are, you had better deliver. Even if they are not, you should still consider what the audience wants out of you. If your boss asked you to give this presentation, your co-workers may cut you a little slack; however, if you suggested this presentation, you will have to work even harder to win everyone over. You should also assess any objections your audience may have to your topic and see how you can work around them.

Which aids will most appeal to them: Is this a techno-savvy crowd that has "been there, done that" with computers, or is it a bunch of people who will find PowerPoint and a digital projector a fascinating new world? To the uninitiated, the old, flashy technology can be a potential distraction. Similarly, younger audience members may not want to work too hard reading traditional aids such as fliers or posters.

If you do not know anything about the audience to which you will be presenting, do some footwork and ask around. Co-workers, business contacts, or presentation organizers should be able to answer your questions as you prepare.

ii. Consider Cultural Considerations

Ignoring cultural differences and expectations is considered rude and inappropriate. It is very important to know their belief systems, values, norms, what they consider ethical and unethical etc. in order to know the kind of language to use and the kind of stories and comics to use for your illustrations.

iii. Interact With Your Audience During Your Talk

All speakers seek to converse with their audience members in order to reach them. As you are delivering your talk, consider adopting a heightened conversational tone.

You could be a super presenter in most respects, but if you can't make your message relate in some way to the lives and experiences of your listeners, you'll never win them over. Just because you may be on the same payroll along with the rest of your co-workers does not mean they will be any more receptive to your presentation, you have to work to make what you say relevant to them, likewise with any other group.

B. Audience Participation

  i. Acknowledge your audience

 ii. Address audience biases (i.e. pre-conceived notions or assumptions carried in the minds of the audience about the subject or the speaker)

iii. Tell the audience why they must take interest in the topic or the subject

166

iv. Allow the audience to actively participate in your delivery process through clapping of hands, shouting, standing, etc.

v. Let them know that their concerns and questions will be addressed at the end of the delivery.

vi. Make conscious effort to obtain feedback

Chapter 19: Starting Is The First Step

Okay, now imagine you're on the stage or in front of the room. What's your opener going to be? Let's go back to "Know Your Audience." Do you want to start with a joke, a quote, a relevant and short story or a statistic? Your presentation should have a common thread that runs through the entire time frame. View your opener as threading the needle. Also, tailor your opener and your presentation to your personality.

Some people are naturally funny and have the ability to deliver material, consistently, with humor. Can you learn to be funny? Absolutely. Iowa State University offers a course called "Comedy College." Comedy is a skill you can learn just like any other skill. Second City, located in Chicago, has a Training Center to help people of all ages hone their skills in improvisational comedy and sketch comedy.

Jokes can be great, but if you don't match it to your audience, it will fall flat. Heart starts racing, breathing is shallow, sweating all over and confidence falters. Remember, you won't die, but you also will not look forward to the next 9 minutes and 15 seconds of your 10-minute presentation. Keep in mind a previous tip: run your joke past somebody you trust to make sure it is appropriate and relevant. And actually funny.

You can't miss with a great quote. Many people in history have said many great, appropriate, and relevant things that should be shared. Here's one for you from Abraham Lincoln: "Always bear in mind that your own resolution to succeed is more important than any other one thing." Abraham Lincoln wrote and delivered one of the most memorable speeches ever. Did you know that the Gettysburg Address was less than 3-minutes long? Did you also know that Abraham Lincoln had an extreme fear of public speaking? **You are not alone**.

A relevant and short story is always a way to reach into the heart of your audience. There were two words: Relevant and SHORT. If you spend too much time with your opener, you could easily cut into the content of your presentation. Even if you have a 6-hour workshop, your opener should be relevant and short.

Did you know that 74% of people have glossophobia? Great statistic. Will your audience know what glossophobia is? You do, because I referred to it earlier in the book. 74% of people have a fear of public speaking. Statistics are a great way to capture your audience. Just be careful that, if you open your presentation with one or two statistics, you don't keep doing it throughout the presentation. Unless, again, it's relevant. Are you talking to a group of college students studying the sciences? Then go crazy with statistics. They love it!

I was teaching a great seminar for leaders that dealt with managing problem employees in Parramatta, Australia on a Friday. Parramatta is a business district in the metropolitan area of Sydney. That weekend, Sydney and Melbourne were slated to play in the Rugby finals.

One thing that is known about Australians: they are serious sports fans. The Aussies have a cheer at sporting events. One half of the crowd yells, "Aussie, Aussie, Aussie"! And the other half yells, "Oy, Oy, Oy"! The next time you are watching any Australian sporting event, I assure you that you will hear this.

I started the day by letting them know I was aware of their upcoming match with Melbourne. I told them I wanted

171

to make sure I was appropriately cheering during the match. I proceeded with "Aussie, Aussie, Aussie." And they, in a resounding noise, yelled, "Oy, Oy, Oy." Their response was so loud, there was feedback on the speakers from my microphone! The Banquet Manager poked his head through the doors to make sure everything was okay. I gave him a thumbs up and he grinned from ear to ear. Even he could tell this was going to be a great day. The entire day remained at that level. To this day, that is still one of my favorite openers to an amazing day!

When choosing your opener, also keep in mind the length of your presentation. Obviously, if you're making a toast to the bride and groom, your opener would simply be explaining how you are connected to them and off you go. In your 10-minute presentation, you might want to break it into three categories. The opener, which will probably be about one to two minutes.

Then the body of the presentation, which will comprise about the next 6 minutes. Then give yourself the last two minutes to wrap it up. That's just an example. You can break that up any way you want to.

If, on the other hand, you are doing a workshop that lasts several hours, or a full-day presentation, you'll want to spend about ten minutes on your opener. In this type of opener, you will build credibility to show the audience why you are the "expert" on the subject and how you plan to keep their attention.

Regardless of how you start, create an opener that will set the tone for the rest of the presentation. During the introduction, I referred to Stephen Covey's habit of "Begin With the End In Mind". If you get stuck on how to open your presentation, you might choose to build the concept of the presentation and decide how you want your presentation to end. Go through the entire process of content and ending, then go back and create your opener.

Chapter 20: Adults Don't Throw Things But They Can Have Attitude

I have enjoyed listening to many personal stories shared by students and delegates over the years. Most are interesting anecdotes that show how many of us share similar lifestyles and challenges. Amongst the shared experiences however are incidents that are embedded in my memory and illustrate the different values and beliefs that can profoundly affect the flow of your presentation. The key is knowing how to react or how not to react and when you just need to move on.

I will share a few stories to illustrate my point.

Scenario One

"Agatha" (not her real name), the cab driver, and the Communication Skills workshop which formed part of an eight week course on Business Administration - for the long-term unemployed.

Many of you will have attended or delivered sessions on 'Communication Skills'. Sender, receiver, message received, message understood, content, clarification, paraphrase, process, engagement. You know the drill. It's been around for years in a variety of forms.

I was in the early stages of a session on verbal communication (e.g. telephone) around how misunderstandings can occur without facial cues to provide fuller meaning. General discussion was underway with students sharing stories of times they were misunderstood through lack of context or other visuals clues to clarify true meaning. It was quite fun and the group was engaged.

Agatha, a heavy-set woman of mature years with strong views, had not been present up to this point but entered a little late, after attending an early morning appointment. (She had recently passed the class on 'A 9am doctor's appointment does not mean you take the whole day off') and was demonstrating competence. On taking her seat at the front of the class I innocently inquired if she had any stories to share about phone calls going wrong.

I soon wished I hadn't asked.

"Well! I'm late because I had to call the unemployment office about my daughter's dole [welfare] payment. They've cut her off and I wanted to know why and the stupid f@#$# bitch on the phone said she couldn't talk to me, only to my daughter. I told her she was a f#$#@ c#$$ and I hung up on her"

Right.

I heard a collective holding of breathe as my brain seized.

I mumbled something that (I think) questioned whether or not she could have used another approach to get the result she was after, and quickly moved on.

The following morning we resumed our Communication Skills studies moving to face-to-face interactions and covered how less than 30% of the communication is about the words themselves – it was all in the tone and body language. I had them enthralled (ok, they were still awake; it was first thing in the morning).

I don't do role plays (as a presenter or student) but encourage sharing of personal experiences, including my own. I'm not sure at what point 'Agatha' joined the class. Evidently I wasn't thinking clearly at the time, overwhelmed and pleased as I was that she had turned up, albeit late again.

As she sat down, I turned to her and asked, "Do you have any examples of a face to face communication that went wrong?"

Really, sometimes I think my brain has a mind of its own, deliberately taking me into minefields to test me.

"Well! I'm late because I had to take my daughter down to the unemployment office as they still haven't made her dole payments. The silly f%$# bitch behind the desk said that there was nothing she could do so I reached across the desk, grabbed her and smacked her in the f%$# face."

Right.

To this day I cannot recall what I said in response but the other students said I did well to recover. I will never know if they were just being kind.

Scenario Two (years later)

A training session on fraud held in a regional town. The room was full to overflowing with front line employees in the public health sector. From the outset it was clear there was an alpha female 'managing' one of the subgroups in the room. The body language was bordering on intimidation. My personal stories were being met with derision and raised eye brows. Clearly the school yard bully had managed to get a job and was continuing her winning ways.

Given the topic, I was a little concerned that the bravado was covering up something more nefarious/malevolent but I had to give the benefit of the doubt. Once I recognised the ring leader I began to ask her opinion of things - addressing her by name. Initially she tried to avoid interaction but as I randomly returned to her she was obliged to respond. The body language changed. I even got a smile (begrudgingly but it was there).

Perhaps she was just misunderstood.

Scenario Three

The delivery of training is sometimes a joint venture. It is a great way to both share the load and have a backup for checking on the arrival of morning tea, the temperature of the room (it never pleases everyone), and other random event management deflections.

The other wonderful thing for trainers who get to team teach is the opportunity to observe the interactions in the room. The stereotypical/archetypal adult student groups might include one or more of the following personalities:

Tell me something I don't know (I bet you can't)

I'm a very busy person (hence my phone is attached to my ear and I will leave the room multiple times to prove it).

Don't expect me to participate in anything remotely fun (you can't make me).

The prolific note-taker

How could you know anything helpful (you don't work here and don't have to put up with the hopeless management)? The facilitator wants to, but doesn't, retort with "I appreciate your feelings, but wonder if you are the problem" - oops - perhaps a bit harsh but it is the thought in my head.

And then there is the nitpicker (a rare but interesting species) and their range of sub-categories, including the:

You aren't following the handout (often true but I like to adjust for the learning requirements in the room as each group is different).

You have a typo (thanks I shouldn't have missed that, will fix for next time).

Your statistics/data/date/place/whatever are incorrect (I apologise and happy to be corrected - please let me know where I would find the correct whatever)

This would not be necessary if the government/organisation had the correct policies, threw money at it, and listened to me, blah, blah, blah. (So off topic but you're not going to let this go are you).

I generally don't have much trouble handling the nitpicker as I just acknowledge their input, appreciate it is important to them, and agree that we could certainly fix the team, company, country, politicians or environment now if only time permitted. Then I casually suggest we need to get on with the session to ensure we finish on time — their time, and yours, is valuable.

However, I have worked with and witnessed a couple of presenters who take this kind of nitpicking as a personal slight and feel they must address the nit face to face - now. The interaction usually gathers steam and the conversation turns a touch argumentative and edges towards personal attacks. The remainder of the attendees start eye rolling and, if the debate grows, they will start to get fidgety and then resentful.

While I advocate assertiveness as a means to ensuring I am not railroaded or bullied into a corner, I am not interested in conversations with people who want to be centre stage by expressing views that are so far outside the purpose of the day. Derailing my class or presentation is not an option. Not because I don't value a personal viewpoint on world economics, local politics or believe that my content is the bee's knees. It's just that I am paid to deliver a certain outcome, for the majority in the room they just want me to get on with it and so do I. They, and I, have a life.

Besides some people like;

a good argument (it's not personal)

a good argument (it is personal)

putting you on the spot so they get kudos with their mates

to show they are smarter than you

Thank you for your input – but I'm about to play your game.

Fortunately, there are some wonderfully helpful people who will give you constructive advice in private. Bless.

Side note; no matter what your presentation is about or how good your presentation is, someone will have a different point of view. Sometimes you will just have to cop it and move on. Learning is constant. Using statistics is an example. If you use stats or data ensure you have a reference to back it up. While most people let numbers float by them, there are some who will be on their smart phones searching Google in a flash and will use this very open forum to correct you! As I have a terrible habit of quoting figures, sayings and other random bits of stuff I've heard somewhere if it fits the moment, my response is simple. "Thank you. I'll look that up." Secretly I am pleased that they were so attentive to my content that they bothered to check up on me!

If you are delivering to a group who all belong to the same organisation, know something about how the organisation works. For example, if you are teaching "Effective Performance Reviews" know what form or process is the minimum requirement. In-house sessions generally require some customisation to ensure consistency with internal policies and procedures.

I have hired many speakers who have spent hours with me prior to a conference to ensure they can connect with internal politics, etc. Generally this has meant that the content of the speech incorporates small elements particular to us, the client. The audience appreciates the connections. Having said that there have also been a very small number of highly paid presenters I have hired who took the time to find out more about the organisation prior -

however, disappointingly, that knowledge was not evident on the day.

Lesson 6 - How to avoid the "smarty pants" ruining your presentation

Have a resource list or links for those who care or want more information

Quote sources for stats, models, theories, etc. on slides or in workbooks

Avoid taking it personally

Chapter 21: Tailoring Your Speech To Connect With The Audience

Every speech is aimed at an audience. Tailoring your speech to connect with the audience is just as important as what is contained in the speech. Many people do not know how to connect with the listeners so that the message meets their expectations and needs. There are many people who do business and never bother to find out any information about their listeners. This makes what may be a great speech become useless because it was not applicable or relevant to the audience.

There are several strategies that one should follow in order to improve presentation skills. You should do proper research before making speeches. The more you know your listeners the higher the chances of passing a message to them effectively. You should find the average age of the crowd that you are going to address. It is also advisable to find out how the gender is split. You can also research on the occupations of the people you are looking forward to addressing.

All this information will help you to engage the group. Sometimes the information may be provided for you but other times you are required to carry out the research yourself. After finding out who the listeners are then you should proceed to finding out what they want. You can start by finding out key issues that impact on the group you are targeting. You can get this information from event organizers.

Another way to find this out is to ask as many listeners as possible. You can do this before the presentation. Most people will tell you what they expect to gain from the presentation. Try to figure out specific wants. After knowing the wants of the group then you should prepare to provide them with that. This will ensure that you win the crowd.

You can also enhance your connection with the listeners by using examples. Nothing builds rapport and empathy better than examples. Examples make ideas tangible, believable, and easy to remember. It is also advisable to use vignettes or short stories. Remember that vignettes should be easy to tell and remember. They should therefore be relevant to the audience to connect with them.

Use of metaphors is also a powerful technique you can use. Metaphors are words which are powerful and they paint clear images in the brains of the listeners. They are a powerful technique used in speech-writing. They are guaranteed to make concepts which are intangible more sensible to the listeners.

You should also be very specific to enhance the connection between you and the listeners. The more you are specific with case studies, results and actual examples the more you will be able to engage the crowd. You should use laser like precision to deliver the message. You should master your content. Feel free to give stories that are personal as examples in the speech. This will enhance the relationship with the crowd.

It is important to make sure that you reinforce the benefit of what you are presenting. This will definitely have an impact on the listeners. Tailoring your speech to connect with the audience is important to make sure your presentation delivers the message.

Chapter 22: Get Over Stage Fright

Many people get nervous before a big presentation, business meeting, or an upcoming date. Nervousness can get the best of us and can be hard to avoid for some, but with some practice, anyone can overcome it. Follow a few simple steps to overcome nervousness about a big event or in daily life.

Visualize your success. Imagine that your presentation will go well. Positive thoughts can help decrease some of your negativity about your social performance and relieve some anxiety.

Get support.

Join a group that offers support for people who have difficulty with public speaking. One effective resource is Toastmasters, a nonprofit organization with local chapters that focuses on training people in speaking and leadership skills.

Know Your Material

Nothing is worse for nerves than trying to give a presentation on a topic you are not well prepared for. This doesn't mean you have to be an expert beforehand, but you'd better know it backward on presentation day. And making sure you've understood your audience and their needs properly will help you ensure that your material is on target to meet their needs.

Know yourself

Try to learn more about your fear or anxiety. Keep an anxiety diary or thought record to note down when it happens and what happens. You can try setting yourself small, achievable goals for facing your fears.

Take Small Steps Moving Forward

Take action using small progressive steps. Please keep in mind that you might at times take a step back. That's okay; just don't get too concerned about this. Keep your head up and stay focused on your desired outcome. Just keep moving forward, and you will eventually get through this, and as a result, gain valuable experience that will ease your nerves the next time around.

Meet and Greet.

Do your best to chat with people before your presentation. Talking with audiences makes you seem more likable and approachable. Ask event attendees questions and take in their responses. They may even give you some inspiration to weave into your talk.

Exercise. Exercise earlier in the day prior to your presentation to boost endorphins, which will help alleviate anxiety

Know your strengths. Write down your strengths, skills, and achievements. There's a reason you've been asked into the room. Regardless of how you feel, most likely you *are* the right person. And it was probably someone more senior, experienced or specialized who invited you to this meeting or to give this presentation. Even if you can't trust your own judgment about whether you're the right person for the role, trust their experience and belief that you are.

Reduce nervous movements. Even if you feel nervous try not to fidget around nervously.

Meditate

If you're frustrated and depressed because of things that happened in the past and nothing worked to change your feelings towards it, you need to start meditating. Find stillness, remain calm and take long breathes. With meditation, you get to keep yourself away from the busy and fast-paced noisy world. You keep yourself away from distractions and make yourself at ease with meditation.

Chapter 23: The Zone

"I'm telling you man, I was in the Zone. Wow! It was just all coming through me. It was like all I had to do was open my mouth and magic came out."

Overheard every other night at Toastmasters

The Zone: The unexplainable, timeless state that exists for writers, athletes and performers when spirit takes over, when body and mind are channels of co-creative bliss.

Jack's New Edge Dictionary

A word about the Zone. For audience and performer, this is the place where all the good stuff happens. You hear athletes talk about the Zone. Jack Nicklaus describes the Zone for golfers this way. "I'm pulling the driver back and I can already see the track of the ball leave the tee before I hit it. I just hit the ball on the path that's already there." Writers get into the Zone and the writing seems to be channeled. They don't have to force it. It happens *through* them. (Aside: it's a misnomer to actually have a non-fiction book category called "Channeled Books." All books are in a large part channeled. In way too many cases, instead of "Channeled Books," the category should be "Unedited Books.")

Performers thrive in the Zone. For many of us, it's what we live for, it's why we do it. When a performer or speaker is in the Zone, the audience is too. Everybody in the room can feel it, even if they can't name it.

There's no real formula for the Zone — sometimes it happens, sometimes it doesn't — but the closest a performer can get to pretending a formula is the *Holy Trio*:

1) Content: knowledge of topic

2) Connection: audience embrace *and*

3) Comfort: being in *the present*.

In other words, the Zone and Communion are virtually the same thing.

OK, enough said about the principles of Communion. At the top of the Communion Trio is Content, meaning, eventually you do have to actually cobble together a speech. If you're wondering how to do that, read on.....

II WRITING
The Point...the Point...the Point
◊ **CONTENT**
 "If you're coming from the heart,
you have the right to speak the truth."
Jack's New Edge Book of Pithy Quotes

"Do not say all that you know,
but know all that you say."
Claudius
• **Know Your Subject**
I can't emphasize enough the importance of being familiar with your

subject. Knowing your subject gives the freedom and permission to dissolve the wall between you and the audience, to tune into the present moment and to trust the outcome.

• Focus/Direction/Momentum

We're getting on a bus, the bus is going to Happy Valley and we're going to whoop it up while we go there.

A speaker (or any performer) is responsible for *direction* — what is the subject? — *focus* — how are we going to get there? and *momentum* — what's our tempo? Keep this in mind while we explore the subject matter. The Communion paradigm assumes that the audience holds your words and thoughts, and the more you tune into them, the easier it is to feed you what we all want to hear in that moment. Still, you have pre-decided what your subject is, and you are the filter (Focus/Direction/Momentum) for the audience.

So, what do you want to share with an audience?

Conclusion

Thank you again for downloading this book!

I hope this book was able to help you to understand how to improve your communication skills, be an effective communicator, and learn to talk with people from all walks of life.

The next step is to follow the steps mentioned in this book, practice, and sooner or later, you'd be the best communicator you can be!

Thank you and good luck!